UNITED NATIONS ORGANIZATION ASSESSMENT: GLOBAL POLITICS, RELATIONS & FUNCTIONS

Andreas Sofroniou, 2021 © Copyright

UNITED NATIONS ORGANIZATION: ASSESSMENT OF GLOBAL POLITICS, RELATIONS & FUNCTIONS

Andreas Sofroniou

Contents   Page

Andreas Sofroniou

Andreas Sofroniou

United Nations flag emblem

The symbol of the United Nations appears on the United Nations flag. It shows a map of the world seen from the North Pole, surrounded by a wreath of olive branches, which represents peace.

The design was officially adopted in 1947.

Andreas Sofroniou

UN, the international organisation

The United Nations as an international organization was established on October 24, 1945.

The United Nations was the second multipurpose international organization established in the 20th century that was worldwide in scope and membership.

Its predecessor, the League of Nations, was created by the Treaty of Versailles in 1919 and disbanded in 1946.

Headquartered in New York City, the UN also has offices in Geneva, Vienna, and other cities.

Its official languages are Arabic, Chinese, English, French, Russian, and Spanish.

Assessment of the UN political relations and functions

The United Nations is the only global international organization that serves multiple functions in international relations.

The UN was designed to ensure international peace and security, and its founders realized

Andreas Sofroniou

that peace and security could not be achieved without attention to issues of rights—including political, legal, economic, social, environmental, and individual.

Yet the UN has faced difficulties in achieving its goals, because its organizational structure still reflects the power relationships of the immediate post-1945 world, despite the fact that the world has changed dramatically—particularly with respect to the post-Cold War relationship between the United States and Russia and the dramatic increase in the number of independent states.

The UN is a reflection of the realities of international politics, and the world's political and economic divisions are revealed in the voting arrangements of the Security Council, the blocs and cleavages of the General Assembly, the different viewpoints within the Secretariat, the divisions present at global conferences, and the financial and budgetary processes.

Despite its intensively political nature, the UN has transformed itself and some aspects of international politics.

Decolonization was successfully accomplished, and the many newly independent states joined the international community and have helped to shape a new international agenda.

The UN has utilized Charter provisions to develop innovative methods to address peace and security issues.

The organization has tried new approaches to economic development, encouraging the establishment of specialized organizations to meet specific needs.

It has organized global conferences on urgent international issues, thereby placing new issues on the international agenda and allowing greater participation by national states, organisations and individuals.

Not-withstanding its accomplishments, the United Nations still operate under the basic provision of respect for national sovereignty and non-interference in the domestic affairs of states.

The norm of national sovereignty, however, runs into persistent conflict with the constant demand by many in the international community that the UN take a more active role in combating aggression and alleviating international problems.

For example, the United States appealed to the issue of national sovereignty to justify its opposition to the Convention on the Rights of the Child and the International Criminal Court.

Thus it is likely that the UN will continue to be seen by its critics as either too timid or too omnipotent as it is asked to resolve the most pressing problems faced by the world's most vulnerable citizens.

Global relations and the world powers

Modern international law, sometimes called the law of nations, has evolved over the last 400 years.

The three major sources of international law according to Article 38 of the Statute of the International Court of Justice are:

- International conventions or treaties;
- International customs; and the
- General principles of law as recognized by civilized nations.

The Permanent Court of Arbitration was established by the Hague Conferences of 1899 and 1907, and the Permanent Court of International Justice was set up in 1921 and succeeded in 1946 by the International Court of Justice.

Since World War II international organizations such as the UN and its related bodies have

Andreas Sofroniou

contributed to the expansion and increased scope of international law to include:

- Political negotiations,
- Strategic affairs,
- Economic standards,
- Social integrations,
- Communications,
- Negotiations, and
- Environmental matters.

By the early 1990s international law had shown its durability and its flexibility by expanding to cover new areas of international relations, and its efficacy when, through the machinery of the UN, Iraq's aggression against Kuwait in 1990 was effectively repudiated.

Andreas Sofroniou

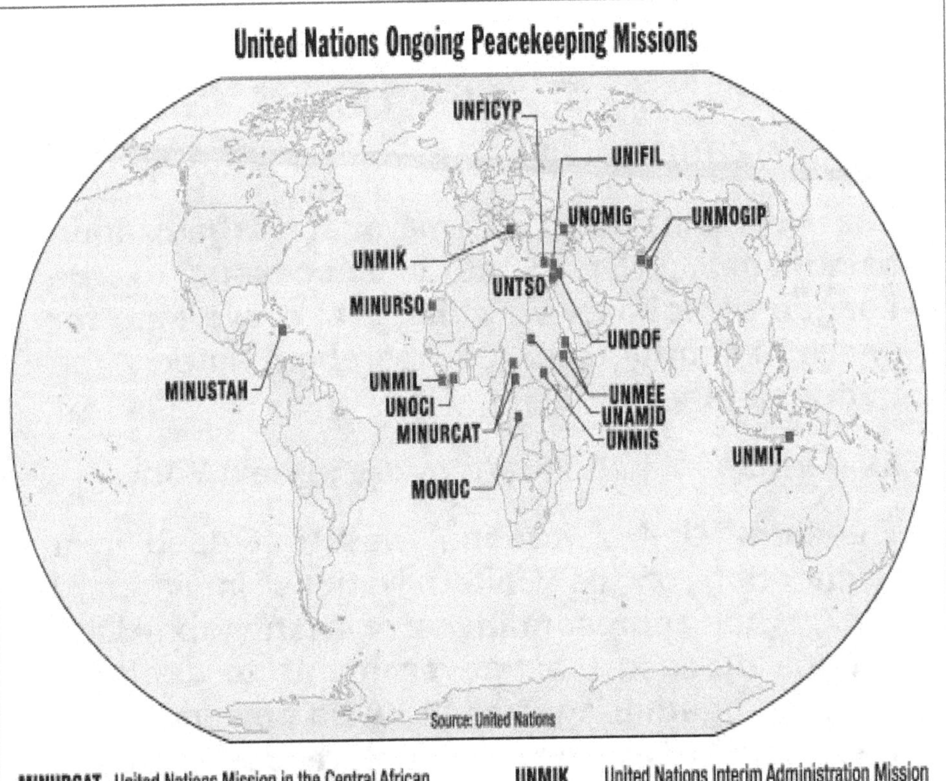

MINURCAT	United Nations Mission in the Central African Republic and Chad; since September 2007 (3)	**UNMIK**	United Nations Interim Administration Mission in Kosovo; since June 1999 (37)[2]
MINURSO	United Nations Mission for the Referendum in Western Sahara; since April 1991 (220)	**UNMIL**	United Nations Mission in Liberia; since September 2003 (15,872)
MINUSTAH	United Nations Stabilization Mission in Haiti; since June 2004 (8,889)	**UNMIS**	United Nations Mission in the Sudan; since March 2005 (10,106)
MONUC	United Nations Organization Mission in the Democratic Republic of the Congo; since November 1999 (18,382)	**UNMIT**	United Nations Integrated Mission in Timor-Leste; since August 2006 (1,496)
UNAMID	United Nations/African Union Hybrid Operation in Darfur; authorized July 2007[1]	**UNMOGIP**	United Nations Military Observer Group in India and Pakistan; since January 1949 (44)
UNDOF	United Nations Disengagement Observer Force (in the Golan Heights); since June 1974 (1,100)	**UNOCI**	United Nations Operation in Côte d'Ivoire; since April 2004 (10,296)
UNFICYP	United Nations Peacekeeping Force in Cyprus; since March 1964 (922)	**UNOMIG**	United Nations Observer Mission in Georgia; since August 1993 (147)
UNIFIL	United Nations Interim Force in Lebanon; since March 1978 (13,264)	**UNTSO**	United Nations Truce Supervision Organization (in Jerusalem); since June 1948 (150)
UNMEE	United Nations Mission in Ethiopia and Eritrea; since July 2000 (1,676)		

Parenthetical figures indicate military and police personnel as of October 31, 2007. [1]Up to 25,987 military and police personnel authorized. [2]2,050 civilian police are also assigned to UNMIK.

11

Background of the United Nations Organization (UN)

The UN is an international organization established in 1945 as a successor to the League of Nations, with the goal of working for peace, security, and co-operation among the nations of the world.

Its permanent headquarters are in New York.

The term 'United Nations' was first used in a Declaration of the United Nations in January 1942, when representatives of twenty-six Allied nations pledged their governments to continue fighting together against the Axis powers, but it was only after further conferences held at Dumbarton Oaks, Washington, in 1944, and San Francisco in 1945 that representatives of fifty Allied countries signed the document, known as the Charter, setting up the new organization.

The UN grew rapidly as newly independent nations, created as a result of decolonization (and latterly as a result of the break-up of the Soviet Union), and applied for membership.

In 1996 the organization had 185 members; an important exception being Switzerland, which maintains a policy of strict neutrality.

Andreas Sofroniou

In order to carry out its many functions, the UN is served by a wide range of organs and institutions.

Six principal organs of the UN

These are the:

1. United Nations General Assembly (UNGA),

2. United Nations Security Council,

3. International Court of Justice,

4. Economic and Social Council (which deals with international economic, social, cultural, educational, health and related matters),

5. Trusteeship Council (which administers those territories held in trust by the UN), and the

6. Secretariat, which is responsible for the general administration of the UN.

The Secretariat is headed by the Secretary-General, appointed for a five-year renewable term by the General Assembly.

Nine Secretary-Generals

There have been nine Secretary-Generals since the UN was founded:

1. Trygve Lie (Norway), 1946-53;

2. Dag Hammarskjold (Sweden), 1953-61;

3. U-Thant (Burma), 1961-71;

4. Kurt Waldheim (Austria), 1971-81;

5. Javier Perez de Cuellar (Peru), 1981-92;

6. Boutros Boutros Ghali (Egypt), 1992-96;

7. Kofi Annan (Ghana), 1996-2006;

8. Ban Koi-moon (South Korea), 2006-2016;

9. Antonio Guterres (Portugal), 2016-Present.

The UN is also served by nineteen inter-governmental agencies known as the specialized agencies, dealing with economic and social questions.

They include the:

- International Atomic Energy Agency (IAEA),

- International Monetary Fund (IMF),

- United Nations Educational, Scientific, and Cultural Organization (UNESCO), and the

- World Health Organization (WHO).

Other organs which are part of the UN system include the:

- United Nations Conference on Trade and Development (UNCTAD), and the

- Office of the United Nations High Commissioner for Refugees (UNHCR).

General Assembly (UNGA)

The United Nations General Assembly (UNGA) is the main deliberative organ of the United Nations Organization, where representatives of every member country sit and have a vote.

The Assembly, based at UN headquarters in New York, can discuss and make recommendations on all questions which fall within the scope of the UN Charter; it is also responsible for the UN budget.

It first met in January 1946 and meets for three months annually in regular session, although both special and emergency sessions can also be convened.

Such sessions have been held to discuss issues of particular importance, such as the Suez crisis in 1956, the Palestinian problem, disarmament, or the sanctioning of the US-led war against Iraq in 1991; or in cases where the United Nations Security Council has failed to agree on a course of action in an international dispute, such as occurred in Afghanistan (1980), Namibia (1981), and the Israeli-occupied Arab territories (1982).

Decisions on important questions require a two-thirds majority; otherwise a simple majority is sufficient. In the UN's early years, the USA could normally command a majority in the General Assembly. But with the dramatic increase in new members following decolonization, the balance shifted to favour the developing countries, which were often unwilling to endorse the policies of either superpower, preferring to adopt a non-aligned stance.

Since the fall of communism in the Soviet Union and Eastern Europe, the General Assembly's numbers have been further swelled by newly independent republics.

At the end of 1996 there were 185 member states.

Andreas Sofroniou

Security Council

The United Nations Security Council is one of the six principal organs of the United Nations Organization, based at UN headquarters in New York, whose prime responsibility is to maintain world peace and security.

The Security Council, which first met in January 1946, consists of five permanent members (the USA, Russia, China, France, and the UK), and ten non-permanent members elected by the United Nations General Assembly for two-year terms on a rotating basis.

With the changes in the economic and political balance of power since the end of the cold war, a change in the permanent membership to admit Germany, Japan, the EU, or other regional powers, is likely to come under discussion.

The Security Council can investigate any international dispute, and recommend ways of achieving a settlement, including 'enforcement measures', such as sanctions, or the use of force by UN members (as, for example, in Somalia in 1992).

It is also responsible for peacekeeping forces such as UNIFIL (United Nations Interim Force in Lebanon), which was established in 1978 to confirm the withdrawal of Israeli forces from

Andreas Sofroniou

southern Lebanon, or **UNIIMOG** (United Nations Iran-Iraq Military Observer Group), established in 1988 to monitor the ceasefire after the Iran-Iraq War.

Decisions taken by the Security Council require a majority of nine, including all five permanent members. This rule of great power unanimity, usually referred to as the right of veto, had been the cause of controversy, as during the cold war, when the activities of the Security Council were frequently paralysed by the failure of the five permanent members to adopt a common position in international crises. The effectiveness of the Council was improved after the collapse of the Soviet bloc in 1991.

By 1992 it was felt by many, including the Secretary-General Dr Boutros Boutros Ghali (1992-), that its membership needed revision to recognize the current world power-structure. The proposal was advanced, in 1994, that permanent Security Council membership be doubled; Germany and Japan made especially strong representations for a permanent seat.

Conference on Trade and Development (UNCTAD)

The United Nations Conference on Trade and Development (UNCTAD) is a permanent agency of the United Nations Organization, with its headquarters in Geneva. It was established in 1964 to promote international trade and economic growth.

The Conference, which meets every four years, called for discrimination in favour of the developing countries, since their industrial products are often subject to quotas and tariffs. UNCTAD has played an important role in devising economic measures to secure advantageous prices for primary commodities and to ensure preferential tariff treatment for developing countries' manufactured goods.

In 1968 it proposed that developed countries should give 1 per cent of their gross national product in aid to developing countries, but the gap between rich and poor countries continued to widen (Brandt Report), aggravated by a steady decline in the price of many basic world commodities which the developing countries produce.

Representatives from 150 countries attended its eighth full session in 1992, when it was agreed that increased emphasis in developing countries on domestic policy reforms and efficiency was needed in a changed international climate.

Rights of the Child

The United Nations Convention on the Rights of the Child is an international treaty, adopted in 1989. The rights apply to all persons under 18 except in countries where the age of majority is lower.

The Convention declares the family to be the natural environment for children, and states that in all actions concerning children account should be taken of their best interests.

It promulgates the child's right to a name and nationality, to privacy, freedom of association, thought, conscience, and religion.

The obligations of others, especially parents and the state are documented. The state, for example, must provide childcare for those with working parents, education, health care, and protection from child sexual exploitation, child abuse and neglect, drug abuse, and child labour.

The treaty indicates the special protections required by vulnerable children such as the victims of armed conflict, handicapped and refugee children, and the children of minorities. It is binding on states which ratify it, but there is no mechanism for enforcement.

Educational, Scientific and Cultural Organization (UNESCO)

The United Nations Educational, Scientific and Cultural Organization (UNESCO) is a specialized agency of the United Nations Organization, founded in 1946 and based in Paris, which promotes international collaboration in education, science, culture, and communication.

In education, it supports the spread of literacy, continuing education, and universal primary education; and in science, assists developing countries, and international interchange between scientists.

It encourages the preservation of monuments and sites, and of other aspects of culture such as oral traditions, music, and dance.

By 1989 UNESCO's 'World Heritage List', designed to protect landmarks of 'outstanding universal value', comprised 315 sites in sixty-seven countries. In the field of communication, UNESCO is committed to the free flow of information. In 1980 its supreme governing body approved a New World Information and Communication

Order despite opposition from those who believed it threatened press freedom. In 1984 the USA (which had been due to supply about a quarter of UNESCO's budget) and in 1985 the UK and Singapore withdrew, alleging financial mismanagement and political bias against Western countries: the UK rejoined in 1997.

High Commissioner for Refugees, Office of the (UNHCR)

The United Nations High Commissioner for Refugees Office of the (UNHCR) is an UN body established in 1951 to replace the International Refugee Organization. The headquarters are in Geneva, and there are five Regional Bureaux.

The UNHCR has four primary functions:

1. Extend international protection to refugees under the terms of the 1951 UN Convention relating to the Status of Refugees;

2. Ensure refugees obtain political asylum and are not forcibly returned to a territory where they fear persecution;

3. Provide emergency relief such as food, shelter, and medical assistance; and

4. Assist in voluntary repatriation, or resettlement and integration into a new community.

Member states

The United Nations member states are the 193 sovereign states that are members of the United Nations (UN) and have equal representation in the UN General Assembly. The UN is the world's largest intergovernmental organization.

The criteria for admission of new members to the UN are set out in Chapter II, Article 4 of the UN Charter:

1. Membership in the United Nations is open to all peace-loving states which accept the obligations contained in the present Charter and, in the judgement of the Organization, are able and willing to carry out these obligations.

2. The admission of any such state to membership in the United Nations will be effected by a decision of the General Assembly upon the recommendation of the Security Council.

A recommendation for admission from the Security Council requires affirmative votes from at least nine of the council's fifteen members, with none of the five permanent members using their veto power. The Security Council's recommendation must then be approved in the General Assembly by a two-thirds majority vote.

In principle, only sovereign states can become UN members and currently all UN members are sovereign states.

Although five members were not sovereign when they joined the UN, all subsequently became fully independent between 1946 and 1991.

Because a state can only be admitted to membership in the UN by the approval of the Security Council and the General Assembly, a number of states that are considered sovereign according to the Montevideo Convention are not members of the UN.

This is because the UN does not consider them to possess sovereignty, mainly due to the lack of international recognition or due to opposition from one of the permanent members.

In addition to the member states, the UN also invites non-member states to become observers at the UN General Assembly (currently two: the Holy See and Palestine), allowing them to participate and speak in General Assembly meetings, but not vote.

Observers are generally inter-governmental organizations and international organizations and entities whose statehood or sovereignty is not precisely defined.

United Nations members

Argentina, Australia, Belarus (Belorussia), Belgium, Bolivia, Brazil, Canada, Chile, China, Colombia, Costa Rica, Cuba, Czechoslovakia, Denmark, Dominican Republic, Ecuador, Egypt, El Salvador, Ethiopia, France, Greece, Guatemala, Haiti, Honduras, India, Iran, Iraq, Lebanon, Liberia, Luxembourg, Mexico, The Netherlands, New Zealand, Nicaragua, Norway, Panama, Paraguay, Peru, Philippines, Poland, Russia (U.S.S.R.)[1], Saudi Arabia, South Africa, Syria, Turkey, Ukraine, United Kingdom, United States, Uruguay, Venezuela, Yugoslavia.

Membership in chronological sequence

1946 Afghanistan, Iceland, Sweden, Thailand

1947 Pakistan, Yemen

1948 Myanmar (Burma)

1949 Israel 1950 Indonesia

1955 Albania, Austria, Bulgaria, Cambodia, Finland, Hungary, Ireland, Italy, Jordan, Laos, Libya, Nepal, Portugal, Romania, Spain, Sri Lanka (Ceylon)

1956 Japan, Morocco, Sudan, Tunisia

1957 Ghana, Malaysia

1958 Guinea

1960 Benin (Dahomey), Burkina Faso (Upper Volta), Cameroon, Central African Republic, Chad, Congo (capital at Brazzaville), Congo (Zaire; capital at Kinshasa), Côte d'Ivoire (Ivory Coast), Cyprus, Gabon, Madagascar, Mali, Niger, Nigeria, Senegal, Somalia, Togo

1961 Mauritania, Mongolia, Sierra Leone, Tanzania[4]

1962 Algeria, Burundi, Jamaica, Rwanda, Trinidad and Tobago, Uganda

1963 Kenya, Kuwait

1964 Malawi, Malta, Zambia

1965 The Gambia, Maldives, Singapore

1966 Barbados, Botswana, Guyana, Lesotho

1968 Equatorial Guinea, Mauritius, Swaziland

1970 Fiji **1971** Bahrain, Bhutan, Oman, Qatar, United Arab Emirates

1973 The Bahamas, Germany[5] 1974 Bangladesh, Grenada, Guinea-Bissau

1975 Cape Verde, Comoros, Mozambique, Papua New Guinea, São Tomé and Príncipe, Suriname

1976 Angola, Samoa, Seychelles

1977 Djibouti, Vietnam

1978 Dominica, Solomon Islands

1979 Saint Lucia

1980 Saint Vincent and the Grenadines, Zimbabwe

1981 Antigua and Barbuda, Belize, Vanuatu

1983 Saint Kitts and Nevis

1984 Brunei

1990 Liechtenstein, Namibia

1991 Estonia, Latvia, Lithuania, Marshall Islands, Micronesia, North Korea, South Korea

1992 Armenia, Azerbaijan, Bosnia and Herzegovina, Croatia, Georgia, Kazakhstan, Kyrgyzstan, Moldova, San Marino, Slovenia, Tajikistan, Turkmenistan, Uzbekistan

1993 Andorra, Czech Republic, Eritrea, Macedonia, Monaco, Slovakia

1994 Palau 1999 Kiribati, Nauru, Tonga

2000 Tuvalu

2002 East Timor, Switzerland

2006 Montenegro

2011 South Sudan

The seat held by the U.S.S.R. was assumed by Russia in 1991.

The Socialist Federal Republic of Yugoslavia was a member from 1945 until its dissolution following the establishment and admission of the new member states of:

Bosnia and Herzegovina, Croatia, Slovenia (1992), Macedonia (1993),

The Federal Republic of Yugoslavia (2000), the last reconstituted as Serbia and Montenegro in 2003.

In 2006 Serbia and Montenegro split into separate countries.

North Yemen (capital at San'a') merged in 1990 with South Yemen (capital at Aden). Upon unification, there was one membership.

Tanganyika merged in 1964 with Zanzibar. The country's name after the merger became Tanzania, with a single UN membership.

East Germany and West Germany were admitted as separate members in 1973. Upon unification of the two countries in 1990, there was one membership.

Czechoslovakia, a member from 1945, split into two countries, the Czech Republic and Slovakia, in 1993.

Current members

The updated list of the current members and their dates of admission are listed on the next page with their official designations used by the United Nations.

The alphabetical order by the member states' official designations is used to determine the seating arrangement of the General Assembly sessions, where a draw is held each year to select a member state as the starting point.

Several members use their full official names in their official designations and thus are sorted out of order from their common names:

- Democratic People's Republic of Korea,

- Democratic Republic of the Congo,

- Republic of Korea,

- Republic of Moldova,

- The Former Yugoslav Republic of Macedonia (a provisional reference used for all purposes within the UN, and listed under T),

- United Republic of Tanzania.

Catalogue of members

Flag	Member state	Date of admission	Notes
	Afghanistan	19 November 1946	
	Albania	14 December 1955	
	Algeria	8 October 1962	
	Andorra	28 July 1993	
	Angola	1 December 1976	

Andreas Sofroniou

Flag	Member state	Date of admission	Notes
	Antigua and Barbuda	**11 November 1981**	
	Argentina	**24 October 1945**	
	Armenia	**2 March 1992**	**Former member: Union of Soviet Socialist Republics**
	Australia	**1 November 1945**	
	Austria	**14 December 1955**	
	Azerbaijan	**2 March 1992**	**Former member: Union of Soviet Socialist Republics**

Flag	Member state	Date of admission	Notes
	Bahamas	18 September 1973	
	Bahrain	21 September 1971	
	Bangladesh	17 September 1974	
	Barbados	9 December 1966	
	Belarus	24 October 1945	Former member: Byelorussian Soviet Socialist Republic
	Belgium	27 December 1945	

Flag	Member state	Date of admission	Notes
	Belize	25 September 1981	
	Benin	20 September 1960	
	Bhutan	21 September 1971	
	Plurinational State of Bolivia	14 November 1945	
	Bosnia and Herzegovina	22 May 1992	Former member: Yugoslavia
	Botswana	17 October 1966	
	Brazil	24 October	

Flag	Member state	Date of admission	Notes
		1945	
	Brunei Darussalam	21 September 1984	
	Bulgaria	14 December 1955	
	Burkina Faso	20 September 1960	
	Burundi	18 September 1962	
	Cabo Verde	16 September 1975	
	Cambodia	14 December 1955	
	Cameroon	20	

Flag	Member state	Date of admission	Notes
		September 1960	
	Canada	9 November 1945	
	Central African Republic	20 September 1960	
	Chad	20 September 1960	
	Chile	24 October 1945	
	China	24 October 1945	Former member: Republic of China
	Colombia	5 November 1945	

Flag	Member state	Date of admission	Notes
	Comoros	12 November 1975	
	Congo	20 September 1960	
	Costa Rica	2 November 1945	
	Côte d'Ivoire	20 September 1960	
	Croatia	22 May 1992	Former member: Yugoslavia
	Cuba	24 October 1945	
	Cyprus	20 September 1960	

36

Flag	Member state	Date of admission	Notes
	Czech Republic	19 January 1993	Former member: Czech oslovakia
	Democratic People's Republic of Korea	17 September 1991	
	Democratic Republic of the Congo]	20 September 1960	
	Denmark	24 October 1945	
	Djibouti	20 September 1977	
	Dominica	18 December 1978	
	Dominican	24 October	

Andreas Sofroniou

Flag	Member state	Date of admission	Notes
	Republic	1945	
	Ecuador	21 December 1945	
	Egypt	24 October 1945	Former member: United Arab Republic
	El Salvador	24 October 1945	
	Equatorial Guinea	12 November 1968	
	Eritrea	28 May 1993	
	Estonia	17 September 1991	Former member: Union of Soviet Socialist Republics
	Ethiopia	13 November 1945	

Flag	Member state	Date of admission	Notes
	Fiji	13 October 1970	
	Finland	14 December 1955	
	France	24 October 1945	
	Gabon	20 September 1960	
	Republic of The Gambia	21 September 1965	
	Georgia	31 July 1992	Former member: Union of Soviet Socialist Republics
	Germany	18 September	Former member: German

Flag	Member state	Date of admission	Notes
		1973	Democratic Republic and Germany
	Ghana	8 March 1957	
	Greece	25 October 1945	
	Grenada	17 September 1974	
	Guatemala	21 November 1945	
	Guinea	12 December 1958	
	Guinea-Bissau	17 September 1974	
	Guyana	20 September	

Flag	Member state	Date of admission	Notes
		1966	
	Haiti	24 October 1945	
	Honduras	17 December 1945	
	Hungary	14 December 1955	
	Iceland	19 November 1946	
	India	30 October 1945	India and the United Nations
	Indonesia	28 September 1950	Withdrawal of Indonesia (1965–1966)
	Islamic Republic of Iran	24 October 1945	

Andreas Sofroniou

Flag	Member state	Date of admission	Notes
	Iraq	21 December 1945	
	Ireland	14 December 1955	
	Israel	11 May 1949	Israel, Palestine,
	Italy	14 December 1955	
	Jamaica	18 September 1962	
	Japan	18 December 1956	Japan and the United Nations
	Jordan	14 December 1955	
	Kazakhstan	2 March 1992	Former member: Union of Soviet

Andreas Sofroniou

Flag	Member state	Date of admission	Notes
			Socialist Republics
	Kenya	16 December 1963	
	Kiribati	14 September 1999	
	Kuwait	14 May 1963	
	Kyrgyzstan	2 March 1992	Former member: Union of Soviet Socialist Republics
	Lao People's Democratic Republic	14 December 1955	
	Latvia	17 September	Former member: Union of Soviet

Flag	Member state	Date of admission	Notes
		1991	Socialist Republics
	Lebanon	24 October 1945	
	Lesotho	17 October 1966	
	Liberia	2 November 1945	
	Libya	14 December 1955	
	Liechtenstein	18 Sept. 1990	
	Lithuania	17 September 1991	Former member: Union of Soviet Socialist Republics
	Luxembour	24 October	Luxembourg

Flag	Member state	Date of admission	Notes
	g	1945	and the United Nations
	Madagascar	20 September 1960	
	Malawi	1 December 1964	
	Malaysia	17 September 1957	Former member: Federation of Malaya
	Maldives	21 September 1965	
	Mali	28 September 1960	
	Malta	1 December 1964	

Flag	Member state	Date of admission	Notes
	Marshall Islands	17 September 1991	
	Mauritania	27 October 1961	
	Mauritius	24 April 1968	
	Mexico	7 November 1945	
	Federated States of Micronesia	17 September 1991	
	Monaco	28 May 1993	
	Mongolia	27 October 1961	
	Montenegro	28 June 2006	Former member: Yugoslavia

Flag	Member state	Date of admission	Notes
	Morocco	12 November 1956	
	Mozambique	16 September 1975	
	Myanmar	19 April 1948	
	Namibia	23 April 1990	
	Nauru	14 September 1999	
	Nepal	14 December 1955	
	Netherlands	10 December 1945	
	New Zealand	24 October 1945	

Flag	Member state	Date of admission	Notes
	Nicaragua	**24 October 1945**	
	Niger	**20 September 1960**	
	Nigeria	**7 October 1960**	
	Norway	**27 November 1945**	
	Oman	**7 October 1971**	
	Pakistan	**30 Sept. 1947**	
	Palau	**15 December 1994**	
	Panama	**13 November 1945**	

Flag	Member state	Date of admission	Notes
	Papua New Guinea	10 October 1975	
	Paraguay	24 October 1945	
	Peru	31 October 1945	
	Philippines	24 October 1945	
	Poland	24 October 1945	
	Portugal	14 December 1955	
	Qatar	21 September 1971	
	Republic of Korea	17 September	

Flag	Member state	Date of admission	Notes
		1991	
	Republic of Moldova	2 March 1992	Former member: Union of Soviet Socialist Republics
	Romania	14 December 1955	
	Russian Federation	24 October 1945	Former member: Union of Soviet Socialist Republics
	Rwanda	18 September 1962	
	Saint Kitts and Nevis	23 September 1983	

Flag	Member state	Date of admission	Notes
	Saint Lucia	18 September 1979	
	Saint Vincent and the Grenadines	16 September 1980	
	Samoa	15 December 1976	
	San Marino	2 March 1992	
	São Tomé and Príncipe	16 September 1975	
	Saudi Arabia	24 October 1945	
	Senegal	28 September 1960	

Flag	Member state	Date of admission	Notes
	Serbia	1 November 2000	Former member: Yugoslavia
	Seychelles	21 September 1976	
	Sierra Leone	27 September 1961	
	Singapore	21 September 1965	Former member: Malaysia and Singapore
	Slovakia	19 January 1993	Former member: Czechoslovakia
	Slovenia	22 May 1992	Former member: Yugoslavia

Flag	Member state	Date of admission	Notes
	Solomon Islands	19 September 1978	
	Somalia	20 September 1960	
	South Africa	7 November 1945	
	South Sudan	14 July 2011	
	Spain	14 December 1955	
	Sri Lanka	14 December 1955	
	Sudan	12 November 1956	
	Suriname	4 December	

Flag	Member state	Date of admission	Notes
		1975	
	Swaziland	24 September 1968	
	Sweden	19 November 1946	
	Switzerland	10 September 2002	
	Syrian Arab Republic	24 October 1945	Former member: United Arab Republic
	Tajikistan	2 March 1992	Former member: Union of Soviet Socialist Republics
	Thailand	16 December 1946	

Flag	Member state	Date of admission	Notes
	The Former Yugoslav Republic of Macedonia	8 April 1993	Former member: Yugoslavia
	Timor-Leste	27 September 2002	
	Togo	20 September 1960	
	Tonga	14 September 1999	
	Trinidad and Tobago	18 September 1962	
	Tunisia	12 November 1956	

Flag	Member state	Date of admission	Notes
	Turkey	24 October 1945	
	Turkmenistan	2 March 1992	Former member: Union of Soviet Socialist Republics
	Tuvalu	5 September 2000	
	Uganda	25 October 1962	
	Ukraine	24 October 1945	Former member: Ukrainian Soviet Socialist Republic
	United Arab Emirates	9 December 1971	

Flag	Member state	Date of admission	Notes
	United Kingdom of Great Britain and Northern Ireland	24 October 1945	
	United Republic of Tanzania	14 December 1961	Former member: Tanganyika and Zanzibar
	United States of America	24 October 1945	
	Uruguay	18 December 1945	
	Uzbekistan	2 March 1992	Former member: Union of Soviet Socialist Republics

Andreas Sofroniou

Flag	Member state	Date of admission	Notes
	Vanuatu	15 September 1981	Vanuatu and the United Nations
	Bolivarian Republic of Venezuela	15 November 1945	
	Vietnam	20 September 1977	
	Yemen	30 September 1947	Former member: Yemen and Democratic Yemen
	Zambia	1 Dec. 1964	
	Zimbabwe	25 August 1980	

Andreas Sofroniou

Permanent five

The permanent members of the United Nations Security Council (also known as the Permanent Five, Big Five, or P5) are the five states which the **UN Charter** of 1945 grants a permanent seat on the **UN Security Council (UNSC)**:

1. **China** (formerly the **Republic of China**),

2. **Russia** (formerly the **Soviet Union**),

3. **France**,

4. **United Kingdom**, and the

5. **United States**.

These countries were all **allies in World War II**, which they won.

They are also all nuclear weapons states.

A total of **15 UN member states** serve on the UNSC, the remainder of which are elected.

Only the five permanent members have the **power of veto**, which enables them to prevent the adoption of any "substantive" draft Council resolution, regardless of its level of international support.

Andreas Sofroniou

Secretariat

This is the organ that administers and coordinates the activities of the United Nations. It is headed by the UN secretary-general.

The Secretariat influences the work of the United Nations to a degree much greater than indicated in the UN Charter. This influence largely results from the fact that the Secretariat's staff is composed of permanent expert officials, rather than political appointees of member nations.

The staff is recruited on a merit basis, with regard to equitable geographic distribution, and its members are required to take an oath of loyalty to the United Nations and are not permitted to receive instructions from their home governments.

The Secretariat's personnel in effect constitute an international civil service. Among them are translators, clerks, technicians, administrators, project directors, and negotiators.

The secretary-general is elected by the General Assembly, on the recommendation of the Security Council, for a renewable five-year term. He must have the approval of all five permanent members of the Security Council to be selected to the post; because of this, secretaries-general have usually come from small, neutral countries.

The secretary-general is the chief administrative officer at all meetings of the General Assembly, the Security Council, the Economic and Social Council, and the Trusteeship Council, and he may carry out any functions that these organs entrust to him and his staff.

He submits an annual report to the General Assembly on the work of the UN, and he may also bring to the Security Council's attention any matter that he deems a threat to international peace and security.

The secretary-general is the chief spokesman for the UN and is that body's most visible and authoritative figure in the arena of world affairs. He has his headquarters at the UN building in New York City.

Andreas Sofroniou

Historical list of UN secretaries-general

–		Gladwyn Jebb (1900–1996)	24 Oct. 1945 – 1 Feb. 1946	U K	Western European & Others	Served as Acting Secretary-General until Lie's election.
	After World War II, he served as Executive Secretary of the Preparatory Commission of the United Nations in August 1945, being appointed Acting United Nations Secretary-General from October 1945 to February 1946 until the appointment of the first Secretary-General, Trygve Lie.				
1		Trygve Lie (1896–1968)	2 Feb. 1946 – 10 Nov. 1952	Norway	Western European & Others	Resigned.
	Lie, a foreign minister and former				

Andreas Sofroniou

labour leader, was recommended by the Soviet Union to fill the post.

After the UN involvement in the Korean War, the Soviet Union vetoed Lie's reappointment in 1951. The United States circumvented the Soviet Union's veto and recommended reappointment directly to the General Assembly.

Lie was reappointed by a vote of 46 to 5, with eight abstentions. The Soviet Union remained hostile to Lie, and he resigned in 1952.

2		Dag Hamma-rskjöld (1905–1961)	10 April 1953 – 18 Sept. 1961	▉▉Swe den	Western European & Others

After a series of candidates were vetoed, Hammarskjöld emerged as an option that was acceptable to the Security Council. He was re-elected unanimously to a second term in 1957.

The Soviet Union was angered by Hammarskjöld's leadership of the UN during the Congo Crisis, and suggested that the position of

Secretary-General be replaced by a troika, or three-man executive.

Facing great opposition from the Western nations, the Soviet Union gave up on its suggestion.

Hammarskjöld died in a plane crash in Northern Rhodesia (now Zambia) in 1961. U.S. President John F. Kennedy called Hammarskjöld "the greatest statesman of our century".

3	U Thant (1909–1974)	30 Nov. 1961 – 31 Dec. 1971	Burma	Asia-Pacific	Declined to stand for a third election.

In the process of replacing Hammarskjöld, the developing world insisted on a non-European and non-American Secretary-General. U Thant was nominated.

However, due to opposition from the French (Thant had chaired a committee on Algerian independence) and the

Arabs (Burma supported Israel),

Thant was only appointed for the remainder of Hammarskjöld's term. He was the first Asian Secretary-General.

The following year, on 30 November, Thant was unanimously re-elected to a new term ending on 3 November 1966. He was re-elected on 2 December 1966, finally for a full 5-year term, ending on 31 December 1971. Thant did not seek a third election.

4		Kurt Waldheim (1918–2007)	1 Jan. 1972 – 31 Dec. 1981	≡Austria	Western European & Others	China vetoed his third term.

Waldheim launched a discreet but effective campaign to become the Secretary-General.

Despite initial vetoes from China and the United Kingdom, in the third round, Waldheim was selected to become the new Secretary-General.

In 1976, China initially blocked Waldheim's re-election, but it relented

Andreas Sofroniou

on the second ballot.

In 1981, Waldheim's re-election for a third term was blocked by China, which vetoed his selection through 15 rounds.

From 1986 to 1992, Waldheim served as President of Austria, making him the first former Secretary-General to rise to the position of head of state. In 1985, it was revealed that a post–World War II UN War Crimes Commission had labelled Waldheim as a suspected war criminal – based on his involvement with the army of Nazi Germany.

The files had been stored in the UN archive.

5		Javier Pérez de Cuéllar (born 1920)	1 Jan. 1982 – 31 Dec. 1991	Peru	Latin American & Caribbean	Did not stand for a third term.

Pérez de Cuéllar was selected after a five-week deadlock between the re-election of Waldheim and China's candidate, Salim   Ahmed

Salim of Tanzania.

Pérez de Cuéllar, a Peruvian diplomat who a decade earlier had served as President of the UN Security Council during his time as Peruvian Ambassador to the UN, was a compromise candidate, and became the first and thus far only Secretary-General from the Americas.

He was re-elected unanimously in 1986.

| 6 | | Boutros Boutros-Ghali (1922–2016) | 1 Jan. 1992 – 31 Dec. 1996 | Egypt | African | The United States vetoed his second term. |

The102-member Non-Aligned Movement insisted that the next Secretary-General come from Africa.

With a majority in the General Assembly and the support of China, the Non-Aligned Movement had the votes necessary to block any unfavourable candidate.

Andreas Sofroniou

		The Security Council conducted five anonymous straw polls—a first for the council—and Boutros-Ghali emerged with 11 votes on the fifth round. In 1996, the United States vetoed the re-appointment of Boutros-Ghali, claiming he had failed in implementing necessary reforms to the UN.[12]			
7		Kofi Annan (born 1938)	1 January 1997 – 31 Dec. 2006	Gha na	African	Retired after two full terms.
		On 13 December 1996, the Security Council recommended Annan. He was confirmed four days later by the vote of the General Assembly. He started his second term as Secretary-General on 1 January 2002.			
8		Ban Ki-moon (born 1944)	1 Jan. 2007 – 31 Dec. 2016	Sou th Korea	Asia-Pacific	Retired after two full terms.

Andreas Sofroniou

Ban became the first East Asian to be selected as the Secretary-General and the second Asian overall after U Thant.

He was unanimously elected to a second term by the General Assembly on 21 June 2011. His second term began on 1 January 2012.

Prior to his selection, he was the Foreign Minister of South Korea from January 2004 to November 2006.

| 9 |  | António Guterres (born 1949) | 1 Jan. 2017 – present | Portugal |

Guterres is the first former head of government to become Secretary-General, and the first Secretary-General born after the establishment of the United Nations.

He was Prime Minister of Portugal from 1995 to 2002.

He has also been President of Socialist International (1999–2005) and United Nations High Commissioner for Refugees (2005–2015).

Andreas Sofroniou

United Nations First session of the General Assembly

First session of the United Nations General Assembly, January 10, 1946, at the Central Hall in London.

Andreas Sofroniou

Aim of the United Nations

According to its Charter, the UN aims to:

- Save succeeding generations from the scourge of war;

- Reaffirm faith in fundamental human rights;

- Establish conditions under which justice and respect for the obligations arising from treaties and other sources of international law can be maintained;

- Promote social progress and better standards of life in larger freedom;

- Maintaining peace and security;

- Developing friendly relations among countries based on respect for the principles of equal rights and self-determination of peoples;

- Achieving worldwide cooperation;

- Solve international economic, social, cultural, and humanitarian problems;

- Respecting and promoting human rights;

- Serving as a centre where countries can coordinate their actions and activities toward these various ends.

Andreas Sofroniou

The UN formed a continuum with the League of Nations in general purpose, structure, and functions; many of the UN's principal organs and related agencies were adopted from similar structures established earlier in the century.

In some respects, however, the UN constituted a very different organization, especially with regard to its objective of maintaining international peace and security and its commitment to economic and social development.

Changes in the nature of international relations resulted in modifications in the responsibilities of the UN and its decision-making apparatus.

Cold War tensions between the United States and the Soviet Union deeply affected the UN's security functions during its first 45 years.

Extensive post-World War II decolonization in Africa, Asia, and the Middle East increased the volume and nature of political, economic, and social issues that confronted the organization.

The Cold War's end in 1991 brought renewed attention and appeals to the UN. Amid an increasingly volatile geopolitical climate, there were new challenges to established practices and functions, especially in the areas of conflict resolution and humanitarian assistance.

Andreas Sofroniou

At the beginning of the 21st century, the UN and its programs and affiliated agencies struggled to address humanitarian crises and civil wars, unprecedented refugee flows, the devastation caused by the spread of AIDS, global financial disruptions, international terrorism, and the disparities in wealth between the world's richest and poorest peoples.

History and development

Despite the problems encountered by the League of Nations in arbitrating conflict and ensuring international peace and security prior to World War II, the major Allied powers agreed during the war to establish a new global organization to help manage international affairs.

This agreement was first articulated when U.S. President Franklin D. Roosevelt and British Prime Minister Winston Churchill signed the Atlantic Charter in August 1941.

The name United Nations was originally used to denote the countries allied against Germany, Italy, and Japan. On January 1, 1942, 26 countries signed the Declaration by United Nations, which set forth the war aims of the Allied powers.

Andreas Sofroniou

The United States, the United Kingdom, and the Soviet Union took the lead in designing the new organization and determining its decision-making structure and functions. Initially, the "Big Three" states and their respective leaders (Roosevelt, Churchill, and Soviet premier Joseph Stalin) were hindered by disagreements on issues that foreshadowed the Cold War.

The Soviet Union demanded individual membership and voting rights for its constituent republics, and Britain wanted assurances that its colonies would not be placed under UN control. There also was disagreement over the voting system to be adopted in the Security Council, an issue that became famous as the "veto problem."

The first major step toward the formation of the United Nations was taken August 21–October 7, 1944, at the Dumbarton Oaks Conference, a meeting of the diplomatic experts of the Big Three powers plus China (a group often designated the "Big Four") held at Dumbarton Oaks, an estate in Washington, D.C.

Although the four countries agreed on the general purpose, structure, and function of a new world organization, the conference ended amid continuing disagreement over membership and voting.

At the Yalta Conference, a meeting of the Big Three in a Crimean resort city in February 1945,

Roosevelt, Churchill, and Stalin laid the basis for charter provisions delimiting the authority of the Security Council.

Moreover, they reached a tentative accord on the number of Soviet republics to be granted independent memberships in the UN.

Finally, the three leaders agreed that the new organization would include a trusteeship system to succeed the League of Nations mandate system.

The Dumbarton Oaks proposals, with modifications from the Yalta Conference, formed the basis of negotiations at the United Nations Conference on International Organization (UNCIO), which convened in San Francisco on April 25, 1945, and produced the final Charter of the United Nations.

The San Francisco conference was attended by representatives of 50 countries from all geographic areas of the world:

- 9 from Europe,

- 21 from the Americas,

- 7 from the Middle East,

- 2 from East Asia,

- 3 from Africa,

Andreas Sofroniou

- 1 each from the Ukrainian Soviet Socialist Republic and the Belorussian Soviet Socialist Republic (in addition to the Soviet Union itself),

- 5 from British Commonwealth countries,

- Poland, which was not present at the conference, was permitted to become an original member of the UN.

Security Council veto power (among the permanent members) was affirmed, though any member of the General Assembly was able to raise issues for discussion.

Other political issues resolved by compromise were the role of the organization in the:

- Promotion of economic and social welfare;

- Status of colonial areas and the distribution of trusteeships;

- Status of regional and defence arrangements; and Great Power dominance versus the equality of states.

The UN Charter was unanimously adopted and signed on June 26 and promulgated on October 24, 1945.

Andreas Sofroniou

Organization and administration

Principles and membership

The purposes, principles, and organization of the United Nations are outlined in the Charter.

The essential principles underlying the purposes and functions of the organization are listed in Article 2 and include the following:

- The UN is based on the sovereign equality of its members;

- Disputes are to be settled by peaceful means;

- Members are to refrain from the threat or use of force in contravention of the purposes of the UN;

- Each member must assist the organization in any enforcement actions it takes under the Charter;

- States that are not members of the organization are required to act in accordance with these principles insofar as it is necessary to maintain international peace and security.

Andreas Sofroniou

Article 2 also stipulates a basic long-standing norm that the organization shall not intervene in matters considered within the domestic jurisdiction of any state.

Although this was a major limitation on UN action, over time the line between international and domestic jurisdiction has become blurred.

New members are admitted to the UN on the recommendation of the Security Council and by a two-thirds vote of the General Assembly.

Often, however, the admittance of new members has engendered controversy. Given Cold War divisions between East and West, the requirement that the Security Council's five permanent members (sometimes known collectively as the P-5)—China, France, the Soviet Union (whose seat and membership were assumed by Russia in 1991), the United Kingdom, and the United States—concur on the admission of new members at times posed serious obstacles.

By 1950 only 9 of 31 applicants had been admitted to the organization. In 1955 the 10th Assembly proposed a package deal that, after modification by the Security Council, resulted in the admission of 16 new states (4 eastern European communist states and 12 non-communist countries).

The most contentious application for membership was that of the communist People's Republic of China, which was placed before the General Assembly and blocked by the United States at every session from 1950 to 1971.

Finally, in 1971, in an effort to improve its relationship with mainland China, the United States refrained from blocking the Assembly's vote to admit the People's Republic and to expel the Republic of China (Taiwan); there were 76 votes in favour of expulsion, 35 votes opposed, and 17 abstentions.

As a result, the Republic of China's membership and permanent Security Council seat were given to the People's Republic.

Controversy also arose over the issue of "divided" states, including the Federal Republic of Germany (West Germany) and the German Democratic Republic (East Germany), North and South Korea, and North and South Vietnam.

The two German states were admitted as members in 1973; these two seats were reduced to one after the country's reunification in October 1990.

Vietnam was admitted in 1977, after the defeat of South Vietnam and the reunification of the country in 1975. The two Koreas were admitted separately in 1991.

Following worldwide decolonization from 1955 to 1960, 40 new members were admitted, and by the end of the 1970s there were about 150 members of the UN.

Another significant increase occurred after 1989–90, when many former Soviet republics gained their independence.

By the early 21st century the UN comprised nearly 190 member states.

United Nations has six principal organs:

1. General Assembly,

2. Security Council,

3. Economic and Social Council,

4. Trusteeship Council,

5. International Court of Justice, and the

6. Secretariat.

General Assembly

The only body in which all UN members are represented, the General Assembly exercises deliberative, supervisory, financial, and elective functions relating to any matter within the scope of the UN Charter.

Andreas Sofroniou

Its primary role, however, is to discuss issues and make recommendations, though it has no power to enforce its resolutions or to compel state action.

Other functions include admitting new members; selecting members of the Economic and Social Council, the non-permanent members of the Security Council, and the Trusteeship Council; supervising the activities of the other UN organs, from which the Assembly receives reports; and participating in the election of judges to the International Court of Justice and the selection of the secretary-general.

Decisions usually are reached by a simple majority vote. On important questions, however—such as the admission of new members, budgetary matters, and peace and security issues—a two-thirds majority is required.

The Assembly convenes annually and in special sessions, electing a new president each year from among five regional groups of states.

At the beginning of each regular session, the Assembly also holds a general debate, in which all members may participate and raise any issue of international concern.

Most work, however, is delegated to six main committees:

(1) Disarmament and International Security,

(2) Economic and Financial,

(3) Social, Humanitarian, and Cultural,

(4) Special Political and Decolonization,

(5) Administrative and Budgetary, and

(6) Legal.

The General Assembly has debated issues that other organs of the UN have either overlooked or avoided, including decolonization, the independence of Namibia, apartheid in South Africa, terrorism, and the AIDS epidemic.

The number of resolutions passed by the Assembly each year has climbed to more than 350, and many resolutions are adopted without opposition. Nevertheless, there have been sharp disagreements among members on several issues, such as those relating to the Cold War, the Arab-Israeli conflict, and human rights.

The General Assembly has drawn public attention to major issues, thereby forcing member governments to develop positions on them, and it has helped to organize ad hoc bodies and conferences to deal with important global problems.

The large size of the Assembly and the diversity of the issues it discusses contributed to the emergence of regionally based voting blocs in the 1960s.

During the Cold War the Soviet Union and the countries of Eastern Europe formed one of the most cohesive blocs, and another bloc comprised the United States and its Western allies.

The admission of new countries of the Southern Hemisphere in the 1960s and '70s and the dissipation of Cold War tensions after 1989 contributed to the formation of blocs based on "North-South" economic issues—i.e., issues of disagreement between the more prosperous, industrialized countries of the Northern Hemisphere and the poorer, less industrialized developing countries of the Southern Hemisphere.

Other issues have been incorporated into the North-South divide, including Northern economic and political domination, economic development, the proliferation of nuclear weapons, and support for Israel.

Security Council

The UN Charter assigns to the Security Council primary responsibility for the maintenance of international peace and security.

The Security Council originally consisted of 11 members—five permanent and six non-permanent—elected by the General Assembly for two-year terms. From the beginning, non-permanent members of the Security Council were elected to give representation to certain regions or groups of states.

As membership increased, however, this practice ran into difficulty. An amendment to the UN Charter in 1965 increased the council's membership to 15, including the original five permanent members plus 10 non-permanent members.

Among the permanent members, the People's Republic of China replaced the Republic of China (Taiwan) in 1971, and the Russian Federation succeeded the Soviet Union in 1991.

After the unification of Germany, debate over the council's composition again arose, and Germany, India, and Japan each applied for permanent council seats.

The non-permanent members are chosen to achieve equitable regional representation, five members coming from Africa or Asia, one from eastern Europe, two from Latin America, and two from western Europe or other areas.

Five of the 10 non-permanent members are elected each year by the General Assembly for two-year terms, and five retire each year. The presidency is held by each member in rotation for a period of one month.

Each Security Council member is entitled to one vote. On all "procedural" matters—the definition of which is sometimes in dispute—decisions by the council are made by an affirmative vote of any nine of its members.

Substantive matters, such as the investigation of a dispute or the application of sanctions, also require nine affirmative votes, including those of the five permanent members holding veto power.

In practice, however, a permanent member may abstain without impairing the validity of the decision. A vote on whether a matter is procedural or substantive is itself a substantive question. Because the Security Council is required to function continuously, each member is represented at all times at the UN's headquarters in New York City.

Any country—even if it is not a member of the UN—may bring a dispute to which it is a party to the attention of the Security Council. When there is a complaint, the council first explores the possibility of a peaceful resolution.

International peacekeeping forces may be authorized to keep warring parties apart pending further negotiations. If the council finds that there is a real threat to the peace, a breach of the peace, or an act of aggression (as defined by Article 39 of the UN Charter), it may call upon UN members to apply diplomatic or economic sanctions. If these methods prove inadequate, the UN Charter allows the Security Council to take military action against the offending country.

During the Cold War, continual disagreement between the United States and the Soviet Union coupled with the veto power of the Security Council's permanent members made the Security Council an ineffective institution. Since the late 1980s, however, the council's power and prestige have grown.

Between 1987 and 2000 it authorized more peacekeeping operations than at any previous time. The use of the veto has declined dramatically, though disagreements among permanent members of the Security Council—most notably in 2003 over the use of military force against Iraq—have occasionally undermined the council's effectiveness. To achieve consensus, comparatively informal meetings are held in private among the council's permanent members, a practice that has been criticized by non-permanent members of the Security Council.

In addition to several standing and ad hoc committees, the work of the council is facilitated by the Military Staff Committee, sanctions committees for each of the countries under sanctions, peacekeeping forces committees, and an International Tribunals Committee.

Economic and Social Council

Designed to be the UN's main venue for the discussion of international economic and social issues, the Economic and Social Council (ECOSOC) directs and coordinates the economic, social, humanitarian, and cultural activities of the UN and its specialized agencies.

Established by the UN Charter, ECOSOC is empowered to recommend international action on economic and social issues; promote universal respect for human rights; and work for global cooperation on health, education, and cultural and related areas.

ECOSOC conducts studies; formulates resolutions, recommendations, and conventions for consideration by the General Assembly; and coordinates the activities of various UN programs and specialized agencies.

Most of ECOSOC's work is performed in functional commissions on topics such as human rights, narcotics, population, social development, statistics, the status of women, and science and technology; the council also oversees regional commissions for Europe,

Asia and the Pacific, Western Asia, Latin America, and Africa.

The UN Charter authorizes ECOSOC to grant consultative status to non-governmental organizations (NGOs).

Three categories of consultative status are recognized:

- General Category NGOs (formerly category I) include organizations with multiple goals and activities;

- Special Category NGOs (formerly category II) specialize in certain areas of ECOSOC activities;

- and Roster NGOs have only an occasional interest in the UN's activities.

Consultative status enables NGOs to attend ECOSOC meetings, issue reports, and occasionally testify at meetings. Since the mid-1990s, measures have been adopted to increase the scope of NGO participation in ECOSOC, in the ad hoc global conferences, and in other UN activities. By the early 21st century, ECOSOC had granted consultative status to more than 2,500 NGOs.

Originally, ECOSOC consisted of representatives from 18 countries, but the Charter was amended in 1965 and in 1974 to increase the number of members to 54.

Members are elected for three-year terms by the General Assembly.

Four of the five permanent members of the Security Council—the United States, United Kingdom, Soviet Union (Russia), and France—have been re-elected continually because they provide funding for most of ECOSOC's budget, which is the largest of any UN subsidiary body. Decisions are taken by simple majority vote.

Trusteeship Council

The Trusteeship Council was designed to supervise the government of trust territories and to lead them to self-government or independence.

The trusteeship system, like the mandate system under the League of Nations, was established on the premise that colonial territories taken from countries defeated in war should not be annexed by the victorious powers but should be administered by a trust country under international supervision until their future status was determined.

Unlike the mandate system, the trusteeship system invited petitions from trust territories on their independence and required periodic international missions to the territories.

Andreas Sofroniou

In 1945 only 12 League of Nations mandates remained:

1. Nauru,

2. New Guinea,

3. Ruanda-Urundi,

4. Togoland and Cameroon (French administered),

5. Togoland and Cameroon (British administered),

6. Carolines,

7. Marshallsa,

8. Marianas,

9. Western Samoa,

10. South West Africa,

11. Tanganyika,

12. Palestine.

All these mandates became trust territories except South West Africa (now Namibia), which South Africa refused to enter into the trusteeship system.

The Trusteeship Council, which met once each year, consisted of states administering trust territories, permanent members of the Security Council that did not administer trust territories,

Andreas Sofroniou

and other UN members elected by the General Assembly.

Each member had one vote, and decisions were taken by a simple majority of those present. With the independence of Palau, the last remaining trust territory, in 1994, the council terminated its operations.

No longer required to meet annually, the council may meet on the decision of its president or on a request by a majority of its members, by the General Assembly, or by the Security Council. Since 1994 new roles for the council have been proposed, including administering the global commons (e.g., the seabed and outer space) and serving as a forum for minority and indigenous peoples.

International Court of Justice

The International Court of Justice, commonly known as the World Court, is the principal judicial organ of the United Nations, though the court's origins predate the League of Nations.

The idea for the creation of an international court to arbitrate international disputes arose during an international conference held at The Hague in 1899.

This institution was subsumed under the League of Nations in 1919 as the Permanent

Court of International Justice (PCIJ) and adopted its present name with the founding of the UN in 1945.

The court's decisions are binding, and its broad jurisdiction encompasses "all cases which the parties refer to it and all matters specially provided for in the Charter of the United Nations or in treaties and conventions in force."

Most importantly, states may not be parties to a dispute without their consent, though they may accept the compulsory jurisdiction of the court in specified categories of disputes.

The court may give advisory opinions at the request of the General Assembly or the Security Council or at the request of other organs and specialized agencies authorized by the General Assembly.

Although the court has successfully arbitrated some cases (e.g., the border dispute between Honduras and El Salvador in 1992), governments have been reluctant to submit sensitive issues, thereby limiting the court's ability to resolve threats to international peace and security.

At times countries also have refused to acknowledge the jurisdiction or the findings of the court. For example, when Nicaragua sued the United States in the court in 1984 for mining its harbours, the court found in favour of

Nicaragua, but the United States refused to accept the court's decision.

The 15 judges of the court are elected by the General Assembly and the Security Council voting independently. No two judges may be nationals of the same state, and the judges are to represent a cross section of the major legal systems of the world. Judges serve nine-year terms and are eligible for re-election. The seat of the World Court is The Hague.

Secretariat

The secretary-general, the principal administrative officer of the United Nations, is elected for a five-year renewable term by a two-thirds vote of the General Assembly and by the recommendation of the Security Council and the approval of its permanent members.

Secretaries-general usually have come from small, neutral countries. The secretary-general serves as the chief administrative officer at all meetings and carries out any functions that those organs entrust to the Secretariat; he also oversees the preparation of the UN's budget.

The secretary-general has important political functions, being charged with bringing before the organization any matter that threatens international peace and security.

Andreas Sofroniou

Both the chief spokesperson for the UN and the UN's most visible and authoritative figure in world affairs, the secretary-general often serves as a high-level negotiator.

Attesting to the importance of the post, two secretaries-general have been awarded the Nobel Prize for Peace: Dag Hammarskjöld in 1961 and Kofi Annan, co-recipient with the UN, in 2001.

The Secretariat influences the work of the United Nations to a much greater degree than indicated in the UN Charter. It is responsible for preparing numerous reports, studies, and investigations, in addition to the major tasks of translating, interpreting, providing services for large numbers of meetings, and other work.

Under the Charter the staff is to be recruited mainly on the basis of merit, though there has been a conscious effort to recruit individuals from different geographic regions.

Some members of the Secretariat are engaged on permanent contracts, but others serve on temporary assignment from their national governments.

In both cases they must take an oath of loyalty to the United Nations and are not permitted to receive instructions from member governments.

The influence of the Secretariat can be attributed to the fact that the some 9,000 people on its staff are permanent experts and international civil servants rather than political appointees of member states.

The Secretariat is based in New York, Geneva, Vienna, Nairobi (Kenya) and other locales. It has been criticized frequently for poor administrative practices—though it has made persistent efforts to increase the efficiency of its operations—as well as for a lack of neutrality.

Subsidiary organs

The United Nations network also includes subsidiary organs created by the General Assembly and autonomous specialized agencies.

The subsidiary organs report to the General Assembly or ECOSOC or both.

Some of these organs are funded directly by the UN; others are financed by the voluntary contributions of governments or private citizens.

In addition, ECOSOC has consultative relationships with NGOs operating in economic, social, cultural, educational, health, and related fields.

NGOs have played an increasingly important role in the work of the UN's specialized agencies, especially in the areas of health, peacekeeping, refugee issues, and human rights.

Specialized agencies

The specialized agencies report annually to ECOSOC and often cooperate with each other and with various UN organs. However, they also have their own principles, goals, and rules, which at times may conflict with those of other UN organs and agencies.

The specialized agencies are autonomous insofar as they control their own budgets and have their own boards of directors, who appoint agency heads independently of the General Assembly or secretary-general.

Major specialized agencies and related organs of the UN include the:

- International Labour Organisation (ILO),

- Food and Agriculture Organization of the United Nations (FAO),

- United Nations Educational, Scientific and Cultural Organization (UNESCO),

- World Health Organization (WHO).

Two of the most powerful specialized agencies, which also are the most independent with respect to UN decision making, are the:

- **World Bank and the**

- **International Monetary Fund (IMF).**

The United Nations, along with its specialized agencies, is often referred to collectively as the United Nations system.

Global conferences

Global conferences have a long history in multilateral diplomacy, extending back to the period after World War I, when conferences on disarmament and economic affairs were convened by the League of Nations.

With the UN's establishment after World War II, the number and frequency of global conferences increased dramatically. The trickle of narrowly focused, functional meetings from the early 1950s became a torrent in the 1990s with a series of widely publicized gatherings attended by high-level representatives and several thousands of other participants.

Virtually all matters of international concern have been debated by UN global conferences, including the proliferation of nuclear weapons, small-arms trafficking, racism, overpopulation,

Andreas Sofroniou

hunger, crime, access to safe drinking water, the environment, the role of women, and human rights.

The format and frequency of the conferences have varied considerably over time. The increasing number of meetings has led to complaints of "conference fatigue" by some countries.

Global conferences have served a number of significant functions. Considered "town meetings of the world," they provide an arena for discussion and for the exchange of information.

The conferences take stock of existing knowledge and help to expand it through the policy analyses that they trigger. They also serve as incubators of ideas, raise elite consciousness, and may also identify emerging issues. For example, the dramatic acceleration in the growth of the world's population in the second half of the 20th century was a challenge first identified by conferences organized by the UN in the 1950s and '60s. Global conferences have nurtured public support for solutions to global issues.

Thus, NGOs have played a key role in many of the UN global conferences. At some conferences, the NGOs have organized parallel conferences to discuss the major issues; at others, they have participated alongside government representatives, serving on national delegations and presenting position papers.

Global conferences have faced a number of criticisms. Some observers claim that they are inefficient and too large and unwieldy to set international agendas.

Others argue that they have been captured by different constituencies, of the North or the South, depending on the issue.

Still others contend that such conferences have become too politicized, with the result that unrelated issues are sometimes linked to serve political purposes.

For example, the global conferences on racism in 1978 and 2001, according to these critics, were unduly politicized by declarations asserting a link between racism and Zionism.

Andreas Sofroniou

Administration

Finances

The secretary-general must submit a biennial budget to the General Assembly for its approval. The Charter stipulates that the expenses of the organization shall be borne by members as apportioned by the General Assembly.

The Committee on Contributions prepares a scale of assessments for all members, based on the general economic level and capacity of each state, which is also submitted to the General Assembly for approval.

The United States is the largest contributor, though the proportion of its contributions has declined continually, from some two-fifths at the UN's founding to one-fourth in 1975 and to about one-fifth in 2000.

Other members make larger per capita contributions. The per capita contribution of San Marino, for example, is roughly four times that of the United States.

The U.S. contribution became a controversial issue during the 1990s, when the country refused to pay its obligations in full and objected to the level of funding it was required to provide.

In 1999 the U.S. Congress passed a UN reform bill, and after intense negotiations UN members agreed to reduce the U.S. share of the budget and to increase contributions from other states to make up the shortfall.

When the cost of the special programs, specialized agencies, and peacekeeping operations is added to the regular budget, the total annual cost of the United Nations system increases substantially. (Special programs are financed by voluntary contributions from UN members, and specialized agencies and peacekeeping operations have their own budgets.)

Partly because of a rapid increase in the number of appeals to the UN for peacekeeping and other assistance after the end of the Cold War and partly because of the failure of some member states to make timely payments to the organization, the UN has suffered continual and severe financial crises.

Andreas Sofroniou

Privileges and immunities

A general Convention on the Privileges and Immunities of the United Nations, approved by the General Assembly in February 1946 and accepted by most of the members, asserts that the UN possesses juridical personality.

The convention also provides for such matters as immunity from legal process of the property and officials of the UN. An agreement between the UN and the United States, signed in June 1947, defines the privileges and immunities of the UN headquarters in New York City.

Headquarters

The General Assembly decided during the second part of its first session in London to locate its permanent headquarters in New York. John D. Rockefeller, Jr., donated land for a building site in Manhattan.

Temporary headquarters were established at Lake Success on Long Island, New York. The permanent Secretariat building was completed and occupied in 1951–52. The building providing accommodations for the General Assembly and the councils was completed and occupied in 1952.

Functions

Maintenance of international peace and security

The main function of the United Nations is to preserve international peace and security. Chapter 6 of the Charter provides for the pacific settlement of disputes, through the intervention of the Security Council, by means such as negotiation, mediation, arbitration, and judicial decisions.

The Security Council may investigate any dispute or situation to determine whether it is likely to endanger international peace and security.

At any stage of the dispute, the council may recommend appropriate procedures or methods of adjustment, and, if the parties fail to settle the dispute by peaceful means, the council may recommend terms of settlement.

The goal of collective security, whereby aggression against one member is met with resistance by all, underlies chapter 7 of the Charter, which grants the Security Council the power to order coercive measures—ranging from diplomatic, economic, and military sanctions to the use of armed force—in cases where attempts at a peaceful settlement have failed.

Such measures were seldom applied during the Cold War, however, because tensions between the United States and the Soviet Union prevented the Security Council from agreeing on the instigators of aggression.

Instead, actions to maintain peace and security often took the form of preventive diplomacy and peacekeeping. In the post-Cold War period, appeals to the UN for peacekeeping and related activities increased dramatically, and new threats to international peace and security were confronted, including AIDS and international terrorism.

Notwithstanding the primary role of the Security Council, the UN Charter provides for the participation of the General Assembly and non-member states in security issues.

Any state, whether it is a member of the UN or not, may bring any dispute or situation that endangers international peace and security to the attention of the Security Council or the General Assembly.

The Charter authorizes the General Assembly to "discuss any questions relating to the maintenance of international peace and security" and to "make recommendations with regard to any such questions to the state or states concerned or to the Security Council or to both."

This authorization is restricted by the provision that, "while the Security Council is exercising in respect of any dispute or situation the functions assigned to it in the present Charter, the General Assembly shall not make any recommendation with regard to that dispute or situation unless the Security Council so requests."

By the "Uniting for Peace" resolution of November 1950, however, the General Assembly granted to itself the power to deal with threats to the peace if the Security Council fails to act after a veto by a permanent member.

Although these provisions grant the General Assembly a broad secondary role, the Security Council can make decisions that bind all members, whereas the General Assembly can make only recommendations.

Andreas Sofroniou

Peacekeeping, peacemaking, and peace building

International armed forces were first used in 1948 to observe cease-fires in Kashmir and Palestine.

Although not specifically mentioned in the UN Charter, the use of such forces as a buffer between warring parties pending troop withdrawals and negotiations—a practice known as peacekeeping—was formalized in 1956 during the Suez Crisis between Egypt, Israel, France, and the United Kingdom.

Peacekeeping missions have taken many forms, though they have in common the fact that they are designed to be peaceful, that they involve military troops from several countries, and that the troops serve under the authority of the UN Security Council. In 1988 the UN Peacekeeping Forces were awarded the Nobel Prize for Peace.

During the Cold War, so-called first-generation, or "classic," peacekeeping was used in conflicts in the Middle East and Africa and in conflicts stemming from decolonization in Asia.

Between 1948 and 1988 the UN undertook 13 peacekeeping missions involving generally lightly armed troops from neutral countries other than the permanent members of the

Andreas Sofroniou

Security Council—most often Canada, Sweden, Norway, Finland, India, Ireland, and Italy. Troops in these missions, the so-called "Blue Helmets," were allowed to use force only in self-defence. The missions were given and enjoyed the consent of the parties to the conflict and the support of the Security Council and the troop-contributing countries.

With the end of the Cold War, the challenges of peacekeeping became more complex. In order to respond to situations in which internal order had broken down and the civilian population was suffering, "second-generation" peacekeeping was developed to achieve multiple political and social objectives.

Unlike first-generation peacekeeping, second-generation peacekeeping often involves civilian experts and relief specialists as well as soldiers. Another difference between second-generation and first-generation peacekeeping is that soldiers in some second-generation missions are authorized to employ force for reasons other than self-defence.

Because the goals of second-generation peacekeeping can be variable and difficult to define, however, much controversy has accompanied the use of troops in such missions.

In the 1990s, second-generation peacekeeping missions were undertaken in Cambodia (1991–

93), the former Yugoslavia (1992–95), Somalia (1992–95), and elsewhere and included troops from the permanent members of the Security Council as well as from the developed and developing world (e.g., Australia, Pakistan, Ghana, Nigeria, Fiji, India).

In the former Yugoslav province of Bosnia and Herzegovina, the Security Council created "safe areas" to protect the predominantly Bosniak (Bosnian Muslim) population from Serbian attacks, and UN troops were authorized to defend the areas with force.

In each of these cases, the UN reacted to threats to peace and security within states, sometimes taking sides in domestic disputes and thus jeopardizing its own neutrality.

Between 1988 and 2000 more than 30 peacekeeping efforts were authorized, and at their peak in 1993 more than 80,000 peacekeeping troops representing 77 countries were deployed on missions throughout the world. In the first years of the 21st century, annual UN expenditures on peacekeeping operations exceeded $2 billion.

In addition to traditional peacekeeping and preventive diplomacy, in the post-Cold War era the functions of UN forces were expanded considerably to include peacemaking and peace building. (Former UN secretary-general Boutros Boutros-Ghali described these additional

Andreas Sofroniou

functions in his reports *An Agenda for Peace* [1992] and *Supplement to an Agenda for Peace* [1995].)

For example, since 1990 UN forces have supervised elections in many parts of the world, including Nicaragua, Eritrea, and Cambodia; encouraged peace negotiations in El Salvador, Angola, and Western Sahara; and distributed food in Somalia.

The presence of UN troops in Yugoslavia during the violent and protracted disintegration of that country renewed discussion about the role of UN troops in refugee resettlement. In 1992 the UN created the Department of Peacekeeping Operations (DPKO), which provides administrative and technical support for political and humanitarian missions and coordinates all mine-clearing activities conducted under UN auspices.

The UN's peacekeeping, peacemaking, and peace-building activities have suffered from serious logistical and financial difficulties.

As more missions are undertaken, the costs and controversies associated with them have multiplied dramatically. Although the UN reimburses countries for the use of equipment, these payments have been limited because of the failure of many member states to pay their UN dues.

Andreas Sofroniou

Sanctions and military action

By subscribing to the Charter, all members undertake to place at the disposal of the Security Council armed forces and facilities for military sanctions against aggressors or disturbers of the peace.

During the Cold War, however, no agreements to give this measure effect were concluded. Following the end of the Cold War, the possibility of creating permanent UN forces was revived.

During the Cold War the provisions of chapter 7 of the UN Charter were invoked only twice with the support of all five permanent Security Council members—against Southern Rhodesia in 1966 and against South Africa in 1977.

After fighting broke out between North and South Korea in June 1950, the United States obtained a Security Council resolution authorizing the use of force to support its ally, South Korea, and turn back North Korean forces.

Because the Soviet Union was at the time boycotting the Security Council over its refusal to seat the People's Republic of China, there was no veto of the U.S. measure. As a result, a U.S.-led multinational force fought under the UN banner until a cease-fire was reached on July 27, 1953.

The Security Council again voted to use UN armed forces to repel an aggressor following the August 1990 invasion of Kuwait by Iraq.

After condemning the aggression and imposing economic sanctions on Iraq, the council authorized member states to use "all necessary means" to restore "peace and security" to Kuwait. The resulting Persian Gulf War lasted six weeks, until Iraq agreed to comply with UN resolutions and withdraw from Kuwait.

The UN continued to monitor Iraq's compliance with its resolutions, which included the demand that Iraq eliminate its weapons of mass destruction. In accordance with this resolution, the Security Council established a UN Special Mission (UNSCOM) to inspect and verify Iraq's implementation of the cease-fire terms.

The United States, however, continued to bomb Iraqi weapons installations from time to time, citing Iraqi violations of "no-fly" zones in the northern and southern regions of the country, the targeting of U.S. military aircraft by Iraqi radar, and the obstruction of inspection efforts undertaken by UNSCOM.

The preponderant role of the United States in initiating and commanding UN actions in Korea in 1950 and the Persian Gulf in 1990–91

Andreas Sofroniou

prompted debate over whether the requirements and spirit of collective security could ever be achieved apart from the interests of the most powerful countries and without U.S. control.

The continued U.S. bombing of Iraq subsequent to the Gulf War created further controversy about whether the raids were justified under previous UN Security Council resolutions and, more generally, about whether the United States was entitled to undertake military actions in the name of collective security without the explicit approval and cooperation of the UN.

Meanwhile some military personnel and members of the U.S. Congress opposed the practice of allowing U.S. troops to serve under UN command, arguing that it amounted to an infringement of national sovereignty. Still others in the United States and Western Europe urged a closer integration of United States and allied command structures in UN military operations.

In order to assess the UN's expanded role in ensuring international peace and security through dispute settlement, peacekeeping, peace building, and enforcement action, a comprehensive review of UN Peace Operations was undertaken.

The resulting Brahimi Report (formally the Report of the Panel on United Nations Peace Operations), issued in 2000, outlined the need

Andreas Sofroniou

for strengthening the UN's capacity to undertake a wide variety of missions.

Among the many recommendations of the report was that the UN maintain brigade-size forces of 5,000 troops that would be ready to deploy in 30 to 90 days and that UN headquarters be staffed with trained military professionals able to use advanced information technologies and to plan operations with a UN team including political, development, and human rights experts.

Arms control and disarmament

The UN's founders hoped that the maintenance of international peace and security would lead to the control and eventual reduction of weapons. Therefore the Charter empowers the General Assembly to consider principles for arms control and disarmament and to make recommendations to member states and the Security Council.

The Charter also gives the Security Council the responsibility to formulate plans for arms control and disarmament. Although the goal of arms control and disarmament has proved elusive, the UN has facilitated the negotiation of several multilateral arms control treaties.

Andreas Sofroniou

Because of the enormous destructive power realized with the development and use of the atomic bomb during World War II, the General Assembly in 1946 created the Atomic Energy Commission to assist in the urgent consideration of the control of atomic energy and in the reduction of atomic weapons.

The United States promoted the Baruch Plan, which proposed the elimination of existing stockpiles of atomic bombs only after a system of international control was established and prohibited veto power in the Security Council on the commission's decisions.

The Soviet Union, proposing the Gromyko Plan, wanted to ensure the destruction of stockpiles before agreeing to an international supervisory scheme and wanted to retain Security Council veto power over the commission. The conflicting positions of the two superpowers prevented agreement on the international control of atomic weapons and energy.

In 1947 the Security Council organized the Commission for Conventional Armaments to deal with armaments other than weapons of mass destruction, but progress on this issue also was blocked by disagreement between the Soviet Union and the Western powers.

As a result, in 1952 the General Assembly voted to replace both of these commissions with a new Disarmament Commission. Consisting of the members of the Security Council and Canada, this commission was directed to prepare proposals that would regulate, limit, and balance reduction of all armed forces and armaments;

- Eliminate all weapons of mass destruction; and

- Ensure international control and use of atomic energy for peaceful purposes only.

After five years of vigorous effort and little progress, in 1957 the International Atomic Energy Agency was established to promote the peaceful uses of atomic energy.

In 1961 the General Assembly adopted a resolution declaring the use of nuclear or thermonuclear weapons to be contrary to international law, to the UN Charter, and to the laws of humanity.

Two years later, on August 5, 1963, the Nuclear Test-Ban Treaty was signed by the Soviet Union, the United Kingdom, and the United States. The treaty—to which more than 150 states later adhered—prohibited nuclear tests or explosions in the atmosphere, in outer space, and underwater.

In 1966 the General Assembly unanimously approved a treaty prohibiting the placement of weapons of mass destruction in orbit, on the

Andreas Sofroniou

Moon, or on other celestial bodies and recognizing the use of outer space exclusively for peaceful purposes.

In June 1968 the Assembly approved the Treaty on the Non-Proliferation of Nuclear Weapons, which banned the spread of nuclear weapons from nuclear to non-nuclear powers; enjoined signatory non-nuclear powers, in exchange for technical assistance in developing nuclear power for "peaceful purposes," not to develop or deploy nuclear weapons; and committed the nuclear powers to engage in measures of disarmament.

The treaty represented a significant commitment on the part of more than 140 (now 185) signatory powers to control nuclear weapons proliferation; nevertheless, for many years the treaty, which went into effect in 1970, was not ratified by significant nuclear powers (including China and France) and many "near-nuclear" states (including Argentina, Brazil, Egypt, Israel, Pakistan, and South Africa).

Some of these states signed the treaty in the early 1990s: South Africa signed in 1991, followed by France and China in 1992.

The UN has been active in attempting to eliminate other weapons of mass destruction of a variety of types and in a variety of contexts. In 1970 the General Assembly approved a treaty

Andreas Sofroniou

banning the placement of weapons of mass destruction on the seabed.

A convention prohibiting the manufacture, stockpiling, and use of biological weapons was approved by the Assembly in 1971 and took effect in 1975, though many states have never acceded to it. In 1991 the UN General Assembly passed a resolution on the registration of conventional arms that required states to submit information on major international arms transfers.

During the first several years of the registry, fewer than half of the UN's members submitted the required information; by 2000 about three-fifths of governments filed annual reports. In 1993 the Chemical Weapons Convention, which prohibited the development, production, stockpiling, and use of chemical weapons and called for the destruction of existing stockpiles within 10 years, was opened for signature.

In 1996 the Comprehensive Nuclear-Test-Ban Treaty, which prohibited the testing of nuclear weapons, was signed—though it has not yet entered into force—and two years later a treaty banning the production and export of antipersonnel land mines (Convention on the Prohibition of the Use, Stockpiling, Production and Transfer of Anti-Personnel Mines and on Their Destruction) was concluded.

Despite international pressure, the United States refused to sign both the test ban and the land mine agreements.

Many negotiations on disarmament have been held in Geneva. Negotiations have been conducted by the Ten-Nation Committee on Disarmament (1960); the Eighteen-Nation Committee on Disarmament (1962–68); the Conference of the Committee on Disarmament (1969–78); and the Disarmament Commission (1979–), which now has more than 65 countries as members.

Three special sessions of the General Assembly have been organized on disarmament, and, though the General Assembly sessions have produced little in the way of substantive agreements, they have served to focus public attention on the issue.

In other forums, significant progress has been made on limiting specific types of armaments, such as bacteriologic, chemical, nuclear, and toxic weapons.

Economic welfare and cooperation

The General Assembly, ECOSOC, the Secretariat, and many of the subsidiary organs and specialized agencies are responsible for promoting economic welfare and cooperation in areas such as post-war reconstruction, technical assistance, and trade and development.

Economic reconstruction

The devastation of large areas of the world and the disruption of economic relations during World War II resulted in the establishment (before the UN was founded) of the United Nations Relief and Rehabilitation Administration (UNRRA) in 1943.

The UNRRA was succeeded by the International Refugee Organization, which operated from 1947 to 1951. To assist in dealing with regional problems, in 1947 ECOSOC established the Economic Commission for Europe and the Economic Commission for Asia and the Far East.

Similar commissions were established for Latin America in 1948 and for Africa in 1958. The major work of economic reconstruction, however, was delegated to the International Bank for Reconstruction and Development (World Bank), one of the major financial institutions created in 1944 at the UN Monetary and Financial Conference (commonly known as the Bretton Woods Conference).

Although the World Bank is formally autonomous from the UN, it reports to ECOSOC as one of the UN's specialized agencies. The World Bank works closely with donor countries, UN programs, and other specialized agencies.

Financing economic development

The World Bank is also primarily responsible for financing economic development. In 1956 the International Finance Corporation was created as an arm of the World Bank specifically to stimulate private investment flows.

The corporation has the authority to make direct loans to private enterprises without government guarantees and is allowed to make loans for other than fixed returns. In 1960 the International Development Association (IDA) was established to make loans to less-developed countries on terms that were more flexible than bank loans.

The UN itself has played a more limited role in financing economic development. The General

Assembly provides direction and supervision for economic activities, and ECOSOC coordinates different agencies and programs.

UN development efforts have consisted of two primary activities:

- First, several regional commissions (for Europe, Asia and the Pacific, Latin America, and Africa) promote regional approaches to development and undertake studies and development initiatives for regional economic projects.

- Second, UN-sponsored technical assistance programs, funded from 1965 through the United Nations Development Programme (UNDP), provide systematic assistance in fields essential to technical, economic, and social development of less-developed countries.

Resident representatives of the UNDP in recipient countries assess local needs and priorities and administer UN development programs.

Andreas Sofroniou

Trade and development

After the massive decolonization of the 1950s and early 1960s, less-developed countries became much more numerous, organized, and powerful in the General Assembly, and they began to create organs to address the problems of development and diversification in developing economies.

Because the international trading system and the General Agreements on Tariffs and Trade dealt primarily with the promotion of trade between advanced industrialized countries, in 1964 the General Assembly established the United Nations Conference on Trade and Development (UNCTAD) to address issues of concern to developing countries.

Toward that end, UNCTAD and the Group of 77 less-developed countries that promoted its establishment tried to codify principles of international trade and arrange agreements to stabilize commodity prices.

UNCTAD discussions resulted in agreements on a Generalized System of Preferences, providing for lower tariff rates for some exports of poorer countries, and on the creation of a Common Fund to help finance buffer stocks for commodity agreements.

UNCTAD also has discussed questions related to shipping, insurance, commodities, the transfer of technology, and the means for assisting the exports of developing countries.

The less-developed countries attempted a more concerted and wide-ranging effort to redistribute wealth and economic opportunities through demands for a New International Economic Order, made in 1974 by the Group of 77 (which had become a permanent group representing the interests of less-developed states in the UN and eventually came to include more than 120 states).

Encouraged by the successful demonstration of economic power by the oil-producing countries during the embargo of 1973–74, developing states demanded greater opportunities for development finance, an increase in the percentage of gross national product allocated by the advanced industrialized states to foreign aid, and greater participation in the specialized agencies created to deal with monetary and development issues, including the World Bank and the IMF.

These demands resulted in limited modification of aid flows and of the practices of specialized agencies and produced much greater debate and publicity surrounding development issues. Following the East Asian financial crisis of the late 1990s, UNCTAD and other UN agencies took

Andreas Sofroniou

part in discussions aimed at creating a new international financial architecture designed to control short-term capital flows.

Social welfare and cooperation

The United Nations is concerned with issues of human rights, including the rights of women and children, refugee resettlement, and narcotics control.

Some of its greatest successes have been in the area of improving the health and welfare of the world's population. In the 1990s, despite severe strains on the resources of UN development programs and agencies resulting from massive refugee movements and humanitarian crises, the UN increased its emphasis on social development.

Refugees

After World War II the International Refugee Organization successfully resettled, repatriated, transported, and maintained more than one million European and Asian refugees.

It was abolished in 1952 and replaced by a new international refugee structure. In 1951 ECOSOC drew up, and the General Assembly approved, a Convention Relating to the Status of Refugees.

The United Nations High Commissioner for Refugees (UNHCR) was then appointed and directed to act under this convention, and ECOSOC appointed an Advisory Commission to assist the high commissioner.

The work of the UNHCR has become increasingly important since the late 1980s, involving major relief operations in Africa, Asia (particularly Southeast and Central Asia), Central America, western and central Europe, and the Balkans. At the end of the 1990s approximately 20 million people had been forced to migrate or had fled oppression, violence, and starvation.

The UNHCR works in more than 120 countries and cooperates with more than 450 NGOs to provide relief and to aid in resettlement. For its services on behalf of refugees, the Office of the UNHCR was awarded the Nobel Prize for Peace in 1954 and 1981.

A separate organization, the United Nations Relief and Works Agency for Palestine Refugees in the Near East (UNRWA), administers aid to refugees in the Middle East.

Human rights

Unlike the League of Nations, the United Nations incorporated the principle of respect for human rights into its Charter, affirming respect for human rights and for fundamental freedoms for all without regard to race, sex, language, or religion.

According to the Charter, the General Assembly is charged with initiating studies and making recommendations, and ECOSOC is responsible for establishing commissions to fulfil this purpose.

Consequently, the Commission on Human Rights, originally chaired by Eleanor Roosevelt, was created in 1946 to develop conventions on a wide range of issues, including an international bill of rights, civil liberties, the status of women (for which there is now a separate commission), freedom of information, the protection of minorities, the prevention of discrimination on the grounds of race, sex, language, or religion, and any other human rights concerns.

The commission prepared the nonbinding Universal Declaration of Human Rights, which was adopted by the General Assembly in 1948.

After the declaration, the commission began drafting two covenants, one on civil and political rights and another on economic and cultural rights.

Differences in economic and social philosophies hampered efforts to reach agreement, but the General Assembly eventually adopted the International Covenant on Economic, Social and Cultural Rights and the International Covenant on Civil and Political Rights in 1966.

The covenants, which entered into force in 1976, are known collectively, along with the Universal Declaration of Human Rights, as the international bill of rights. Although all countries have stated support for the 1948 declaration, not all observe or have ratified the two covenants.

In general, Western countries have favoured civil and political rights (rights to life, liberty, freedom from slavery and arbitrary arrest, freedom of opinion and peaceful assembly, and the right to vote), and developing countries have stressed economic and cultural rights such as the rights to employment, shelter, education, and an adequate standard of living.

The Commission on Human Rights and its sub-commission meet annually in Geneva to consider a wide range of human rights issues. Human rights violations are investigated by a

Human Rights Committee set up according to the provisions of the International Covenant on Civil and Political Rights.

The commission and sub-commission also carry out special responsibilities delegated by the General Assembly or by ECOSOC. The commission and sub-commission have strengthened human rights norms and expanded the range of recognized rights, in part by drafting additional conventions on matters such as women's rights, racial discrimination, torture, labour laws, apartheid, and the rights of indigenous peoples.

In particular, the UN has acted to strengthen recognition of the rights of women and children. It established a special Convention on the Elimination of All Forms of Discrimination Against Women, which was approved in 1979 and has been ratified by some 170 countries, and the 1989 Convention on the Rights of the Child, which has been ratified by more than 190 countries.

In 1995 the Fourth World Conference on Women, held in Beijing, developed a Platform for Action to recognize women's rights and improve women's livelihood worldwide, and follow-up meetings monitored progress toward meeting these goals. UNIFEM, the United Nations Development Fund for Women, has

Andreas Sofroniou

worked since 1995 to implement the Beijing Platform for Action.

The UN, through special rapporteurs and working groups, monitors compliance with human rights standards. In 1993 the General Assembly established the post of United Nations High Commissioner for Human Rights (UNHCHR), which is the focal point within the UN Secretariat for human rights activity.

Control of narcotics

The Commission on Narcotic Drugs was authorized by the General Assembly in 1946 to assume the functions of the League of Nations Advisory Committee on Traffic in Opium and Other Dangerous Drugs.

In addition to re-establishing the pre-World War II system of narcotics control, which had been disrupted by the war, the United Nations addressed new problems resulting from the development of synthetic drugs.

Efforts were made to simplify the system of control by drafting one convention incorporating all the agreements in force. The UN established the Office for Drug Control and Crime Prevention (ODCCP) in 1997 to address problems relating to drugs, crime, and international terrorism.

Health and welfare issues

The UN, through the United Nations Children's Fund (UNICEF) and specialized agencies such as the World Health Organization (WHO), works toward improving health and welfare conditions around the world.

UNICEF, originally called the UN International Children's Emergency Fund, was established by the General Assembly in December 1946 to provide for the needs of children in areas devastated by World War II.

UNICEF was made a permanent UN organization in 1953. Financed largely by the contributions of member states, it has helped feed children in more than 100 countries, provided clothing and other necessities, and sought to eradicate diseases such as tuberculosis, whooping cough, and diphtheria. UNICEF promotes low-cost preventive health care measures for children, including the breast-feeding of infants and the use of oral re-hydration therapy to treat diarrhoea, the major cause of death in children. UNICEF has key monitoring responsibilities under the Convention on the Rights of the Child.

WHO is the primary UN agency responsible for health activities. Among its major initiatives have been immunization campaigns to protect populations in the developing world, regulation

Andreas Sofroniou

of the pharmaceutical industry to control the quality of drugs and to ensure the availability of lower-cost generics, and efforts to combat the spread of HIV/AIDS.

The UN has responded to the AIDS epidemic through the establishment of UNAIDS, a concerted program of cosponsoring agencies, including UNICEF, WHO, UNDP, UNESCO, and the World Bank.

UNAIDS is the leading advocate of global action on AIDS, supporting programs to prevent transmission of the disease, providing care for those infected, working to reduce the vulnerability of specific populations, and alleviating the economic and social impact of the disease. In 2001 UNAIDS coordinated a General Assembly special session on the disease.

Andreas Sofroniou

Environment

In response to growing worldwide concern with environmental issues, the General Assembly organized the United Nations Conference on the Human Environment, which was held in Stockholm in 1972 and led to the creation of the United Nations Environment Programme (UNEP) in the same year.

UNEP has attempted to find solutions to various environmental problems, including:

- Pollution in the Mediterranean Sea;

- Threat to aquatic resources posed by human economic activity;

- Deforestation, desertification, and drought;

- Depletion of the Earth's ozone layer by human-produced chemicals; and

- Global warming.

Much disagreement has arisen regarding the scientific bases of environmental concerns and the question of how to combine the goals of environmental protection and development.

Although both developed and developing countries recognize the need to preserve natural resources, developing countries often charge that the environment has been despoiled

Andreas Sofroniou

primarily by the advanced industrialized states, whose belated environmental consciousness now hampers development for other countries.

In other instances, developed countries have objected to the imposition of environmental standards, fearing that such regulations will hamper economic growth and erode their standard of living.

UNEP succeeded in establishing, through the General Assembly, a World Commission on Environment and Development and in 1988 outlined an environmental program to set priorities for the 1990–95 period.

International conferences, such as the United Nations Conference on Environment and Development (the "Earth Summit"), held in Rio de Janeiro in 1992, have continued to focus attention on environmental issues.

The Earth Summit, which was far larger than any previous intergovernmental global conference, incorporated input from numerous NGOs.

It produced a declaration of principles (the Rio Declaration on Environment and Development), a plan for the sustainable development of the Earth's resources into the 21st century (Agenda 21), and guidelines for the management, conservation, and sustainable development of forests.

Andreas Sofroniou

Subsequent UN conferences on social issues continued to incorporate sustainable development policies into their programs.

Dependent areas

The United Nations has expressed concern for people living in non-self-governing territories. Most importantly, the UN has affirmed and facilitated the transition to independence of former colonies.

The anti-colonial movement in the UN reached a high point in 1960, when the General Assembly adopted a resolution sponsored by more than 40 African and Asian states.

This resolution, called the Declaration on the Granting of Independence to Colonial Countries and Peoples, condemned "the subjection of peoples to alien subjugation, domination and exploitation" and declared that "immediate steps shall be taken...to transfer all powers" to the peoples in the colonies "without any conditions or reservations, in accordance with their freely expressed will and desire...in order to enable them to enjoy complete independence and freedom."

After the decolonization period of the 1950s and '60s, new states exerted increasing power and influence, especially in the General Assembly.

With the admission of the new states of Africa and Asia to the United Nations in the 1960s and '70s and the end of the Cold War in 1991, politics within the General Assembly and the Security Council changed as countries formed regional voting blocs to express their preferences and principles.

UN efforts to gain independence for Namibia from South Africa, carried out from the 1940s to the '80s, represent perhaps the most enduring and concerted attempt by the organization to promote freedom for a former colony.

In 1966 the General Assembly took action to end the League of Nations mandate for South West Africa, providing for a United Nations Council for South West Africa in 1967 to take over administrative responsibilities in the territory and to prepare it for independence by 1968.

South Africa refused to acknowledge the council, and the General Assembly, secretary-general, and Security Council continued to exert pressure through the 1970s. In 1978 the General Assembly adopted a program of action toward Namibian independence, and the Security Council developed a plan for free elections.

In 1988, with Namibian independence and the departure of Cuban troops from neighbouring Angola implicitly linked, South Africa finally agreed to withdraw from Namibia. In the following year a UN force—United Nations

Andreas Sofroniou

Temporary Auxiliary Group (UNTAG)— supervised elections and assisted in repatriating refugees. Namibia gained formal independent status in 1990.

Development of international law

The United Nations, like the League of Nations, has played a major role in defining, codifying, and expanding the realm of international law.

The International Law Commission, established by the General Assembly in 1947, is the primary institution responsible for these activities.

The Legal Committee of the General Assembly receives the commission's reports and debates its recommendations; it may then either convene an international conference to draw up formal conventions based on the draft or merely recommend the draft to states.

The International Court of Justice reinforces legal norms through its judgments. The commission and the committee have influenced international law in several important domains, including the laws of war, the law of the sea, human rights, and international terrorism.

The work of the UN on developing and codifying laws of war was built on the previous accomplishments of the Hague Conventions

(1899–1907), the League of Nations, and the Kellog-Briand Pact (1928).

The organization's first concern after World War II was the punishment of suspected Nazi war criminals. The General Assembly directed the International Law Commission to formulate the principles of international law recognized at the Nürnberg trials, in which German war criminals were prosecuted, and to prepare a draft code of offences against the peace and security of mankind.

In 1950 the commission submitted its formulation of the Nürnberg principles, which covered crimes against peace, war crimes, and crimes against humanity. In the following year the commission presented to the General Assembly its draft articles, which enumerated crimes against international law, including any act or threat of aggression, annexation of territory, and genocide.

Although the General Assembly did not adopt these reports, the commission's work in formulating the Nürnberg principles influenced the development of human rights law.

The UN also took up the problem of defining aggression, a task attempted unsuccessfully by the League of Nations. Both the International Law Commission and the General Assembly undertook prolonged efforts that eventually resulted in agreement in 1974.

Andreas Sofroniou

The definition of aggression, which passed without dissent, included launching military attacks, sending armed mercenaries against another state, and allowing one's territory to be used for perpetrating an act of aggression against another state.

In 1987 the General Assembly adopted a series of resolutions to strengthen legal norms in favour of the peaceful resolution of disputes and against the use of force.

The UN has made considerable progress in developing and codifying the law of the sea as well.

The International Law Commission took up the law of the sea as one of its earliest concerns, and in 1958 and 1960, respectively, the General Assembly convened the First and the Second United Nations Conferences on the Law of the Sea (UNCLOS).

The initial conference approved conventions on the continental shelf, fishing, the high seas, and territorial waters and contiguous zones, all of which were ratified by the mid-1960s. During the 1970s it came to be accepted that the deep seabed is the "common heritage of mankind" and should be administered by an international authority.

In 1973 the General Assembly called UNCLOS III to discuss the conflicting positions on this issue as well as on issues relating to navigation, pollution, and the breadth of territorial waters.

The resulting Law of the Sea Treaty (1982) has been ratified by some 140 countries. The original treaty was not signed by the United States, which objected to the treaty's restrictions on seabed mining.

The United States signed a revised treaty after a compromise was reached in 1994, though the agreement has yet to be ratified by the U.S. Senate.

The UN has worked to advance the law of treaties and the laws regulating relations between states. In 1989 the General Assembly passed a resolution declaring 1990–99 the UN Decade of International Law, to be dedicated to promoting acceptance and respect for the principles and institutions of international law.

In 1992 the General Assembly directed the International Law Commission to prepare a draft statute for an International Criminal Court. The Rome Statute of the International Criminal Court (ICC) was adopted in July 1998 and later signed by more than 120 countries.

The ICC, which is to be located at The Hague upon the ratification of the statute by at least 60 signatory countries, has jurisdiction over crimes against humanity, crimes of genocide, war crimes, and crimes of aggression, pending

Andreas Sofroniou

an acceptable definition of that term. Under the terms of the convention, no person age 18 years or older is immune from prosecution, including presidents or heads of state.

Since 1963 the United Nations has been active in developing a legal framework for combating international terrorism.

The General Assembly and specialized agencies such as the International Civil Aviation Organization and the International Atomic Energy Agency established conventions on issues such as offences committed on aircraft, acts jeopardizing the safety of civil aviation, the unlawful taking of hostages, and the theft or illegal transfer of nuclear weapons technology.

In 2001, in the wake of devastating terrorist attacks that killed thousands in the United States, the General Assembly's Ad Hoc Committee on Terrorism continued work on a comprehensive convention for the suppression of terrorism.

Recent events and the United Nations

UN record of main activities

In 2013 the UN coped with the fallout from more turmoil in the Middle East and a further erosion of democratic aspirations from the 'Arab Spring'.

Egyptian Pres. Mohammed Morsi was deposed by the military in July, and Syria kept convulsing in all-out civil war.

Two years after the Palestine state was voted full membership in the United Nations Educational and Cultural Organization (UNESCO) and the U.S. stopped paying its legally binding dues to the agency, the U.S. lost its UNESCO voting privileges.

Saudi Arabia—in a rare move and one that was widely interpreted as a sign of protest against UN inaction in Syria and U.S. policies in Iran, Syria, and elsewhere in the Middle East—turned down the prestigious seat that it had been elected to on the UN Security Council.

The global economic, food, and energy predicaments continued to have a heavy impact on most countries, with the world's poor being hit the hardest.

The number of refugees and internally displaced persons (IDPs) jumped dramatically, especially in the wake of the Syrian crisis.

On the other hand, significant progress was reported in the global fight against HIV/AIDS.

In regard to nuclear proliferation, the International Atomic Energy Agency (IAEA) and Iran signed a Joint Statement on a Framework for Cooperation, and an international Arms Trade Treaty was signed and opened for ratification.

Peace and Security

In 2013 Syria remained arguably the most serious threat to international peace and stability. Civil conflict continued to escalate in the country over the course of the year, and this intensified violence prompted decisive UN action in multiple areas.

Following a chemical weapons strike that killed hundreds of Syrian civilians on August 21, the UN Security Council authorized a joint mission with the Organization for the Prohibition of Chemical Weapons (OPCW) to destroy Syria's chemical weapons.

The UN-OPCW team visited 23 chemical-weapon sites in Syria and destroyed all equipment used to make such weapons. Jerry Smith, head of

OPCW field operations, confirmed that Syria was no longer in a position to produce or use chemical weapons.

The OPCW was awarded the Nobel Prize for Peace for its efforts to destroy these weapons; however, spokespeople for the OPCW said that significant work still remained in this area.

UN Secretary-General Ban Ki-Moon charged that a war crime had been committed and that the international community had a moral responsibility to hold those responsible accountable.

On December 2 the UN High Commissioner for Human Rights said that an inquiry had produced evidence that war crimes had been authorized at the highest level, including by Syrian Pres. Bashar al-Assad.

As of Oct. 31, 2013, the UN Department of Peacekeeping (DPKO) was leading 15 peacekeeping operations and one political mission in Afghanistan, comprising 118,580 personnel, of which 98,014 were in uniform.

More than 50% of the peacekeepers were engaged in two missions: the UN Organization Stabilization Mission in the Democratic Republic of the Congo (MONUSCO), with 26,024 personnel, and the African Union (AU)–UN Hybrid Operation in Darfur (UNAMID), with 23,759.

Some 119 member states contributed uniformed personnel, with the largest contributors being Pakistan (8,285), Bangladesh (7,941), India (7,864), Ethiopia (6,594), Nigeria (4,777), Rwanda (4,622), and Nepal (4,551).

On October 30, amid increasing turmoil and warnings of possible genocide, the Security Council approved a special 250-person military force to the Central African Republic to protect UN workers there.

Also, in November the Security Council authorized a temporary boost of more than 4,000 troops for the AU peacekeeping force in Somalia and approved an expanded UN-support package for logistic support.

In addition to its peacekeeping operations, the UN fielded 13 political and peace-building missions.

Most of the political ones were in Africa, which also hosted three regionally focused missions: the UN Office in Central Africa (UNOCA), the UN Office in West Africa (UNOWA), and the UN Regional Centre for Preventive Diplomacy for Central Asia (UNRCCA). The UN provided assistance in about 50 countries.

Non-proliferation

The UN also pursued several long-standing nuclear non-proliferation goals in 2013, specifically targeting states of historical insecurity such as North Korea and Iran.

In April the second preparatory conference of the parties to the UN-backed Treaty on the Non-proliferation of Nuclear Weapons convened in Geneva.

The conference reaffirmed commitment to nuclear disarmament, non-proliferation, and peaceful uses of nuclear energy. With regard to Iran specifically, some strides were made in 2013 to halt and contain its developing nuclear program, which the Iranian government had claimed was intended for peaceful purposes only.

Despite a rocky start in summer, talks between the IAEA and Iran culminated on November 11 with a Joint Statement on a Framework for Cooperation to strengthen cooperation and communication.

The pact, viewed as a first step, was aimed at providing the IAEA with greater access to Iran's nuclear programs to ensure verification of the peaceful nature of the state's nuclear development program.

Andreas Sofroniou

Regarding North Korea's nuclear program, there were still significant strides to be made. In February North Korea completed its third successful nuclear test.

In addition to its commitment to nuclear non-proliferation, the UN made efforts to curb illegal small-arms proliferation.

In April the UN General Assembly approved and later more than 65 countries signed the Arms Trade Treaty (ATT), which was considered an unprecedented landmark in multilateral small-arms-control efforts.

Though many countries—including the United States—signed the treaty, fewer than 10 signatories had ratified it by year's end.

Humanitarian Aid and Human Rights

According to the UN High Commissioner for Refugees (UNHCR), in 2012 there were more refugees or IDPs than at any other time since 1994. At the end of 2012, more than 45.2 million were displaced, up from 42.5 million the previous year.

Of these, 15.4 million were refugees, 937,000 asylum seekers, and 28.8 million IDPs, the highest level in two decades. Of the refugees, 55% came from five war-torn countries: Afghanistan, Iraq, Somalia, Sudan, and Syria.

During the year 7.6 million became newly displaced. The year ended with 10.5 million refugees under the care of the UNHCR and 4.9 million receiving assistance from the UN Relief and Works Agency for Palestinian Refugees (UNRWA).

An overwhelming number—about 80%—were located in less-developed countries (LDCs) that were ill-equipped to deal with them. Pakistan hosted the largest number of refugees worldwide, with 1.6 million, followed by Iran (868,000) and Germany (589,700).

Much of the humanitarian assistance was provided by the UN to areas affected by intrastate turmoil in the Middle East and Africa. The UN Human Rights Council's primary focus was responding to the humanitarian crisis in Syria, where more than nine million Syrians—about 40% of the population—were in need of humanitarian aid.

The Sahel region of Africa continued to be plagued by pervasive poverty, food insecurity, and civil turmoil. Over the past decade the region had experienced three major droughts, and more than 11 million people were at risk of hunger, with 5 million children under the age of five at risk of acute malnutrition.

The World Bank and the EU pledged more than $8 billion—$1.5 billion and $6.75 billion, respectively—to stimulate economic growth in the region. Two French journalists were kidnapped and assassinated in Mali in 2013, which prompted formal condemnation by the UN and establishment of the Multidimensional Integrated Stabilization Mission in Mali (MINUSMA).

This included authorization of a 12,640-member peacekeeping force. By October 31, 5,872 uniformed personnel had been deployed. MINUSMA's primary goal was to support Mali's political process.

In the Democratic Republic of the Congo (DRC), the Security Council gave approval for a UN intervention force to move against other armed groups. Some 10,000 people in the DRC fled to Uganda after fighting escalated between Congolese government forces and the rebel group M23.

According to UNHCR, attacks occurred near the DRC's border with Uganda, which also was hit by the bombings. As a result, UNHCR began transporting refugees away from the border. The UN announced in December that it would deploy surveillance drones in the DRC to seek out rebel groups.

In the Philippines the UN used more than $25 million from the Central Emergency Response Fund in rapid response to Super Typhoon Haiyan. The storm struck in November and killed more than 5,000 people.

In November the UN General Assembly elected 14 new countries—Algeria, China, Cuba, France, Maldives, Mexico, Morocco, Namibia, Saudi Arabia, South Africa, Macedonia, Vietnam, Russia, and the U.K.—to serve on the UN Human Rights Council beginning in January 2014. The Council had 47 members, and membership was based on geographic distribution.

Millennium Development Goals (MDGs)

As 2013 closed, only two years remained to the MDGs deadline. On the positive side, three important MDG targets had been met: on poverty, slums, and water.

The share of people living on less than $1.25 a day dropped to less than half of its 1990 level—attaining the first MDG target.

Moreover, the poverty rate and the number of people living in extreme poverty fell in every developing region for the first time since poverty monitoring began, and the proportion of people not having access to improved water sources was cut in half from the 1990 level.

In addition, the MDG target was met in 2010 for significantly improving the lives of one million slum dwellers by 2020; more than two million gained access to improved water sources as well as sanitation or had secured durable or less-crowded housing.

Also, the target to reduce by half the percentage of people suffering from hunger was judged within reach. The proportion of undernourished people in LDCs declined from 23.2% in 1990–92 to 14.9% in 2010–12. Significant gains were also made in illness-related deaths—especially from malaria and tuberculosis.

Between 2000 and 2010, mortality rates from malaria fell by more than 25% globally. Death rates from tuberculosis at the global level and in several regions were likely to be halved by 2015 compared with 1990 levels. The number of new HIV infections continued to decline.

However, progress toward other MDG targets—including sanitation, universal primary education, and maternal mortality rates—remained slow and continued to fall far short of 2015 targets.

Andreas Sofroniou

Sustainable Development and Environment

In an effort to limit climate change, the UN hosted (in November) one major multilateral event: the 19th Conference of Parties (COP19) to the United Nations Framework Convention on Climate Change (UNFCCC), which was held in Warsaw.

The conference was attended by government delegates, representatives from business and industry, environmental organizations, research institutions, and media representatives.

Tensions ran high, and compromise proved difficult. Some progress was made on a few issues, such as reducing emissions from deforestation and degradation and financial compensation for LDCs suffering loss and damage from climate change. Also, a timetable was put forward to guide negotiations, looking ahead to a 2015 formal agreement.

Andreas Sofroniou

Health

The UN reported major progress on the HIV/AIDS front. About 2.3 million people were newly infected with HIV in 2012, but this figure was the lowest number since the mid-1990s.

Even more impressive, the number of children newly infected was only 260,000—a 52% drop from 2001. A record number of people—nearly 10 million—in low- and middle-income countries were getting access to antiretroviral drugs in 2012. However, new HIV infections were on the rise in eastern Europe, Central Asia, the Middle East, and North Africa.

Perhaps the health issue of broadest and most universal concern was the shortage of health care professionals, especially in LDCs. The UN World Health Organization (WHO) reported an estimated deficit of 7.2 million health care workers in 2013 and a shortage by 2035 of 12.9 million such workers.

Asia would likely be affected the worst; however, sub-Saharan Africa would probably feel the shortages most severely. For example, within the 47 countries of sub-Saharan Africa, there were only 168 medical schools (24 countries had only one), and 11 countries were without medical schools.

Addressing significant need in the region, the UN brokered an agreement to allow medical and other supplies to be sent to Yemen, which was experiencing a period of significant instability owing to what the UN called a democratic transition. An estimated 13 million Yemenis—more than half of the country's population—required humanitarian relief, particularly medical aid.

The UN approved evacuation of wounded citizens from the northern part of the country. Additionally, Yemeni child malnutrition rates were among the highest in the world; two million Yemeni children were considered "stunted," and one million were deemed acutely malnourished.

In an effort to protect a polio outbreak from spreading in Syria in October, WHO—in collaboration with UNICEF—initiated the largest-ever immunization campaign in the Middle East. This effort targeted children, 20 million of whom would be vaccinated, in eight countries and territories, including Egypt, Iraq, Jordan, Lebanon, Syria, and Turkey, as well as in the West Bank and the Gaza Strip.

Within Syria's borders alone, the campaign reached 1.6 million children with vaccines against polio, measles, mumps, and rubella. Continued surveillance was necessary to detect

Andreas Sofroniou

future outbreaks early and to prevent a possible spread.

Acknowledging the need for women's and children's health services, Secretary-General Ban urged officials to pursue the MDG that ensures the universal provision of health services to women and children—including reproductive-health and family-planning services. He noted that worldwide 200 million women and girls did not have access to family-planning services. He expressed hope and confidence that these challenges could be met by WHO.

Administration, Finance, and Reform

For the 2012–13 bienniums, the UN's budget was cut to $5.15 billion from the previous $5.41 billion. This reduction represented only the second time in 50 years that the UN's regular budget had been slashed.

The total approved peacekeeping budget was set at $7.54 billion for the period July 1, 2013–June 30, 2014. As of Oct. 31, 2013, member states owed $3.26 billion in unpaid peacekeeping dues—up from the $1.76 billion owed a year earlier.

Imminent demands for the UN

Precious political freedom

Freedom is the condition in which people, individually or collectively, can control their own lives without interference either by other people or by some outside political authority.

In the modern world, the demand for political freedom takes two main forms:

- The demand of nations that they should throw off foreign rule, and govern themselves through their own political institutions; and

- The demand of individuals that the state should not interfere in areas of life that are deemed to be private.

This last demand includes specific freedoms such as freedom of expression and worship, freedom of association, and (more controversially) economic freedom in the sense of the freedom to buy, sell, and contract with any willing party.

Political philosophers such as Isaiah Berlin ('Two Concepts of Liberty', 1958) have drawn a distinction between negative and positive senses of freedom, where being negatively free

Andreas Sofroniou

means simply not being prevented or deterred by other people from achieving one's goals, whereas being positively free means having the capacity (the resources, the mental determination, and so on) to achieve those goals.

Freedom, although an important political value, must be limited for its own sake and for the sake of other ends. The best-known principle for deciding this is enunciated in Mill's essay On Liberty (1859): people should be free to act as they like except when their actions cause harm to other people.

Freedom of expression

Freedom of expression (free speech) is the right of every individual to free expression of his or her opinions, including the right to receive or impart information through any medium.

It is one of the basic human rights, included in the Universal Declaration on Human Rights and the European Convention on Human Rights, and enshrined in the First Amendment to the US Constitution.

Freedom of expression is regarded as a fundamental part of the democratic process, assisting the emergence of the truth, as well as providing a means of self-fulfilment for the individual.

The term implies freedom of conscience and religion, the freedom of the press, and free participation in political activity, none of which are tolerated in totalitarian societies.

However, even in democratic societies, freedom of expression is not an absolute right. It can be curtailed by considerations of national security, or subject to laws relating to privacy, defamation, pornography, incitement to racial hatred, contempt of court, protection of confidences, and copyright.

Freedom of information

Freedom of information is the principle that information held by state authorities should be available to the public.

In most Western democratic countries other than the UK there is legislation which requires state agencies, and sometimes private bodies, to make files available to people with a legitimate interest in seeing them, subject to restrictions necessary to protect competing interests, such as national security, and the privacy and commercial rights of others.

Freedom of information encourages democratic accountability by making possible informed

Andreas Sofroniou

debate by citizens and legislatures of public policy and government performance, and by allowing people the right to check the accuracy of records held about them. Under totalitarian regimes, information is rigidly controlled.

Citizens have no right to investigate or challenge government activities. Even demographic information (on population movements or patterns of disease, for example) may be suppressed.

Information and speculation about individuals gathered through informers, the secret services, and, often, technological surveillance is never open to public scrutiny.

Free will

Free will is referred to the philosophical problem of understanding how it is possible for people to be held morally responsible for their actions, given that there is reason for thinking that what they do is determined by causes.

The problem of free will originates in the context of theology: if God is omniscient and omnipotent, it appears to follow that everything people do is foreknown by God, and determined by God's will.

The same problem, in a secular context, is often seen in terms of a clash between morality and science: whereas moral practices (such as punishment) require our actions to be free, science tells us that everything we do is governed by the inexorable laws of nature; the deterministic view is of the world, including people, as just a vast machine, all of whose movements could in principle, given enough information, be predicted by physical science.

Two important views of the nature of free will are those of the libertarian and the compatibilist. Libertarians, such as Kant, hold that free will consists in the ability to do otherwise than one in fact does, that is, power of choice, and that this involves a suspension of the laws of nature.

Libertarians have difficulty in explaining how this is possible, and Kant thought that for there to be free will, people had to be thought of as being in some sense outside the bounds of nature.

Compatibilists such as Hume, by contrast, deny that this much is needed for free will. They hold instead that a person acts freely so long as he is not constrained by external forces, such as the will of another person.

For a compatibilist it is enough for a person to have acted freely that he knew what he was doing and that his action expressed his desires or character.

Andreas Sofroniou

Compatibilists face in turn the problem of explaining why the factors which determine a person's desires or character, such as their genetic make-up or upbringing, over which they have no control, should not be regarded as depriving them of free will.

International covenant for the UN

Civil and Political Rights

International Covenant on Civil and Political Rights is a covenant adopted by the UN in 1966. Eighty-eight countries are signatories.

The covenant promulgates the civil and political rights enumerated in the Universal Declaration of Human Rights of 1948. Whereas the Declaration is not legally binding, the covenant has the legal force of a treaty for the parties to it.

The rights safeguarded include freedom of expression, conscience, and movement; the right to liberty and privacy, the right to vote, and the right to a fair trial.

These rights are to apply without discrimination, and legal remedies are to be available within each state against breaches of the covenant. Signatories undertake to respect its provisions and to submit reports to a human rights committee within the UN.

This committee is also responsible for a procedure through which states, and, in certain circumstances, individuals, may complain of non-compliance.

By comparison with the International Covenant on Economic, Social and Cultural Rights adopted in the same year, this covenant is more specific in its delineation of rights, stronger in affirming states' obligations, and better provided with means of review and supervision.

Andreas Sofroniou

Recent conflicts requiring the UN immediate attention

Recent religious conflicts around the world and frequent invasions of powerful countries into other peoples' territories, makes life even more difficult for the people who are pursuing equality, the application of International Human Rights, and the solutions to conflicts.

The most recent announcement of North Korea, that it started the disarmament of nuclear weapons, will definitely need peace negotiations and a great deal of initiative from the United Nations and the various sections of the organisation.

Of an equally important attention are the various accusations and indecisiveness regarding the agreement with Iran and its nuclear power development plans.

It is very difficult for me, as an author and a firm advocate of peace and freedom, to write about the International Rights for the Human Races, Women, Children, Families, Animals, Religions, Politics, Gay Movements, Wars, Freedom, Democracy and Free Will, their Conflicts and all their Legal implications.

Therefore, in writing this book I tried to include real life experiences and draw from history, institutions, and recent events, worldwide.

Also, in order to justify the contents of a manuscript of this kind I borrowed from examples of how people survive poverty, family conflicts, invasion, war, escape, ethnic cleansing, people misplacement, migration, refugee camps, and recession.

Finally, a plea to the United Nations Organisation, the world leaders, and the professionals of the world; in these restless times you as leaders, continue your support for harmony to all people.

END

Andreas Sofroniou

Index   Page

Andreas Sofroniou

Andreas Sofroniou

Andreas Sofroniou

Bibliography

ALL BOOKS LISTED BELOW ARE PUBLISHED BY ANDREAS SOFRONIOU

1. THERAPEUTIC PSYCHOLOGY, ISBN: 978-1-326-34523-5

2. MEDICAL ETHICS THROUGH THE AGES, ISBN: 978-1-4092-7468-1

3. MEDICAL ETHICS, FROM HIPPOCRATES TO THE 21ST CENTURY ISBN: 978-1-4457-1203-1

4. MISINTERPRETATION OF SIGMUND FREUD, ISBN: 978-1-4467-1659-5

5. JUNG'S PSYCHOTHERAPY: THE PSYCHOLOGICAL & MYTHOLOGICAL METHODS, ISBN: 978-1-4477-4740-6

6. FREUDIAN ANALYSIS & JUNGIAN SYNTHESIS, ISBN: 978-1-4477-5996-6

7. ADLER'S INDIVIDUAL PSYCHOLOGY AND RELATED METHODS, ISBN: 978-1-291-85951-5

8. ADLERIAN INDIVIDUALISM , JUNGIAN SYNTHESIS, FREUDIAN ANALYSIS, ISBN: 978-1-291-85937-9

9. PSYCHOTHERAPY, CONCEPTS OF TREATMENT, ISBN: 978-1-291-50178-0

10. PSYCHOLOGY, CONCEPTS OF BEHAVIOUR, ISBN: 978-1-291-47573-9

11. PHILOSOPHY FOR HUMAN BEHAVIOUR, ISBN: 978-1-291-12707-2

12. SEX, AN EXPLORATION OF SEXUALITY, EROS AND LOVE, ISBN: 978-1-291-56931-5

13. PSYCHOLOGY FROM CONCEPTION TO SENILITY, ISBN:

978-1-4092-7218-2

14. PSYCHOLOGY OF CHILD CULTURE, ISBN: 978-1-4092-7619-7

15. JOYFUL PARENTING, ISBN: 0 9527956 1 2

16. GUIDE TO A JOYFUL PARENTING, ISBN: 0 952 7956 1 2

17. THERAPEUTIC PHILOSOPHY FOR THE INDIVIDUAL AND THE STATE, ISBN: 978-1-4092-7586-2

18. PHILOSOPHIC COUNSELLING FOR PEOPLE AND THEIR GOVERNMENTS, ISBN: 978-1-4092-7400-1

19. CHILD PSYCHOTHERAPY, ISBN: 978-1-326-44169-2

20. HYPNOTHERAPY IN MEDICINE, PSYCHOLOGY, MAGIC, ISBN: 978-1-326-48163-6

21. ART FOR PSYCHOTHERAPY, ISBN: 978-1-326-78959-6

22. SLEEPING AND DREAMING EXPLAINED BY ARTS & SCIENCE, ISBN: ISBN: 978-1-326-81309-3

23. PHILOSOPHY AND POLITICS, ISBN: 978-1-326-33854-1

24. MORAL PHILOSOPHY, FROM SOCRATES TO THE 21ST AEON, ISBN: 978-1-4457-4618-0

25. MORAL PHILOSOPHY, FROM HIPPOCRATES TO THE 21ST AEON, ISBN: 978-1-84753-463-7

26. MORAL PHILOSOPHY, THE ETHICAL APPROACH THROUGH THE AGES, ISBN: 978-1-4092-7703-3

27. MORAL PHILOSOPHY, ISBN: 978-1-4478-5037-3

28. 2011 POLITICS, ORGANISATIONS, PSYCHOANALYSIS, POETRY, ISBN: 978-1-4467-2741-6

29. WISDOM AN ACCUMULATION OF KNOWLEDGE, ISBN: 978-1-326-99692-5

Andreas Sofroniou

30. MYTHOLOGY LEGENDS FROM AROUND THE GLOBE, ISBN: 978-1-326-98630-8

31. PLATO'S EPISTEMOLOGY, ISBN: 978-1-4716-6584-4

32. ARISTOTLE'S AETIOLOGY, ISBN: 978-1-4716-7861-5

33. MARXISM, SOCIALISM & COMMUNISM, ISBN: 978-1-4716-8236-0

34. MACHIAVELLI'S POLITICS & RELEVANT PHILOSOPHICAL CONCEPTS, ISBN: 978-1-4716-8629-0

35. BRITISH PHILOSOPHERS, 16TH TO 18TH CENTURY, ISBN: 978-1-4717-1072-8

36. ROUSSEAU ON WILL AND MORALITY, ISBN: 978-1-4717-1070-4

37. EPISTEMOLOGY, A SYSTEMATIC OVERVIEW, ISBN: 978-1-326-11380-3

38. HEGEL ON IDEALISM, KNOWLEDGE & REALITY, ISBN: 978-1-4717-0954-8

39. METAPHYSICS FACTS AND FALLACIES, ISBN: 978-1-326-80745-0

40. SOCIAL SCIENCES AND PHILOLOGY, ISBN: 978-1-326-33840-4

41. PHILOLOGY, CONCEPTS OF EUROPEAN LITERATURE, ISBN: 978-1-291-49148-7

42. THREE MILLENNIA OF HELLENIC PHILOLOGY, ISBN: 978-1-291-49799-1

43. CYPRUS, PERMANENT DEPRIVATION OF FREEDOM, ISBN: 978-1-291-50833-8

44. SOCIOLOGY, CONCEPTS OF GROUP BEHAVIOUR, ISBN: 978-1-291-51888-7

45. SOCIAL SCIENCES, CONCEPTS OF BRANCHES AND

Andreas Sofroniou

RELATIONSHIPS ISBN: 978-1-291-52321-8

46. CONCEPTS OF SOCIAL SCIENTISTS AND GREAT THINKERS, ISBN: 978-1-291-53786-4

47. EMPIRES AND COLONIALISM ISBN: 978-1-326-46761-6

48. CYPRUS, COLONISED BY MOST EMPIRES, ISBN, 978-1-326-47164-4

49. PERICLES, GOLDEN AGE OF ATHENS, ISBN: 978-1-326-47592-5

50. TRIANGLE OF EDUCATION TRAINING EXPERIENCE, ISBN: 978-1- 326-82934-6

51. HARMONY IS LOVE FRIENDSHIP SEX, ISBN: 978-1-326-85687-8

52. INTERNATIONAL HUMAN RIGHTS, ISBN: 978-1-326-87348-6

53. ANALYSIS OF LOGIC AND SANITY, ISBN: ISBN: 978-1-326-90604-7

54. INTERNATIONAL LAW, GLOBAL RELATIONS, WORLD POWERS, ISBN: 978-1-326-92921-3

55. MANAGEMENT SCIENCE AND BUSINESS, ISBN: 978-1-326-45508-8

56. ECONOMICS WORLD HOUSE RULES, ISBN: 978-1-326-96162-6

57. POLITICAL SYSTEMS NORMS AND LAWS, ISBN: 978-1-326-97404-6

58. HISTORY OF SYSTEMS, ENGINEERING, TECHNOLOGY, ISBN: 978-1-326-94420-9

59. INFORMATION TECHNOLOGY AND MANAGEMENT, ISBN: 978-1-326-34496-2

60. I.T. RISK MANAGEMENT, ISBN: 978-1-4467-5653-9

Andreas Sofroniou

61. SYSTEMS ENGINEERING, ISBN: 978-1-4477-7553-9

62. BUSINESS INFORMATION SYSTEMS, CONCEPTS AND EXAMPLES, ISBN: 978-1-4092-7338-7

63. A GUIDE TO INFORMATION TECHNOLOGY, ISBN: 978-1-4092-7608-1

64. CHANGE MANAGEMENT IN I.T., ISBN: 978-1-4092-7712-5

65. FRONT-END DESIGN AND DEVELOPMENT FOR SYSTEMS APPLICATIONS, ISBN: 978-1-4092-7588-6

66. I.T RISK MANAGEMENT, ISBN: 978-1-4092-7488-9

67. I.T. RISK MANAGEMENT – 2011 EDITION, ISBN: 978-1-4467-5653-9

68. SIMPLIFIED PROCEDURES FOR I.T. PROJECTS DEVELOPMENT, ISBN: 978-1-4092-7562-6

69. SIGMA METHODOLOGY FOR RISK MANAGEMENT IN SYSTEMS DEVELOPMENT, ISBN: 978-1-4092-7690-6

70. TRADING ON THE INTERNET IN THE YEAR 2000 AND BEYOND, ISBN: 978-1-4092- 7577

71. STRUCTURED SYSTEMS METHODOLOGY, ISBN: 978-1-4477-6610-0

72. INFORMATION TECHNOLOGY LOGICAL ANALYSIS, ISBN: 978-1-4717-1688-1

73. I.T. RISKS LOGICAL ANALYSIS, ISBN: 978-1-4717-1957-8

74. LOGICAL ANALYSIS OF I.T. CHANGES, ISBN: 978-1-4717-2288-2

75. LOGICAL ANALYSIS OF SYSTEMS, RISKS , CHANGES, ISBN: 978-1-4717-2294-3

76. COMPUTING, A PRÉCIS ON SYSTEMS, SOFTWARE AND

Andreas Sofroniou

HARDWARE, ISBN: 978-1-2910-5102-5

77. MANAGE THAT I.T. PROJECT, ISBN: 978-1-4717-5304-6

78. CHANGE MANAGEMENT, ISBN: 978-1-4457-6114-5

79. MANAGEMENT OF COMMERCIAL COMPUTING, ISBN: 978-1-4092-7550-3

80. PROGRAMME MANAGEMENT WORKSHOP, ISBN: 978-1-4092-7583-1

81. MANAGEMENT OF I.T. CHANGES, RISKS, WORKSHOPS, EPISTEMOLOGY, ISBN: 978-1-84753-147-6

82. THE PHILOSOPHICAL CONCEPTS OF MANAGEMENT THROUGH THE AGES, ISBN: 978-1-4092- 7554-1

83. MANAGEMENT OF PROJECTS, SYSTEMS, INTERNET, AND RISKS, ISBN: 978-1-4092- 7464-3

84. HOW TO CONSTRUCT YOUR RESUMÊ, ISBN: 978-1-4092-7383-7

85. DEFINE THAT SYSTEM, ISBN: 978-1-291-15094-0

86. INFORMATION TECHNOLOGY WORKSHOP, ISBN: 978-1-291-16440-4

87. CHANGE MANAGEMENT IN SYSTEMS, ISBN: 978-1-4457-1099-0

88. SYSTEMS MANAGEMENT, ISBN: 978-1-4710-4907-1

89. TECHNOLOGY, A STUDY OF MECHANICAL ARTS AND APPLIED SCIENCES, ISBN: 978-1-291-58550-6

90. EXPERT SYSTEMS, KNOWLEDGE ENGINEERING FOR HUMAN REPLICATION, ISBN: 978-1-291- 59509-3

91. ARTIFICIAL INTELLIGENCE AND INFORMATION TECHNOLOGY, ISBN: 978-1-291- 60445-0

92. PROJECT MANAGEMENT PROCEDURES FOR SYSTEMS DEVELOPMENT, ISBN: 978-0-952-72531-2

Andreas Sofroniou

93. SURFING THE INTERNET, THEN, NOW, LATER. ISBN: 978-1--291-77653-9

94. ANALYTICAL DIAGRAMS FOR I.T. SYSTEMS, ISBN: 978-1-326-05786-2

95. INTEGRATION OF INFORMATION TECHNOLOGY, ISBN: 978-1-312-64303-1

96. TRAINING FOR CHANGES IN I.T. ISBN: 978-1-326-14325-1

97. WORKSHOP FOR PROJECTS MANAGEMENT, ISBN: 978-1-326-16162-0

98. SOFRONIOU COLLECTION OF FICTION BOOKS, ISBN: 978-1-326-07629-0

99. THE TOWERING MISFEASANCE, ISBN: 978-1-4241-3652-0

100. DANCES IN THE MOUNTAINS – THE BEAUTY AND BRUTALITY, ISBN: 978-1-4092-7674-6

101. YUSUF'S ODYSSEY, ISBN: 978-1-291-33902-4

102. WILD AND FREE, ISBN: 978-1-4452-0747-6

103. HATCHED FREE, ISBN: 978-1-291-37668-5

104. THROUGH PRICKLY SHRUBS, ISBN: 978-1-4092-7

105. BLOOMIN' SLUMS, ISBN: 978-1-291-37662-3

106. SPEEDBALL, ISBN: 978-1-4092-0521-0

107. SPIRALLING ADVERSARIES, ISBN: 978-1-291-35449-2

108. EXULTATION, ISBN: 978-1-4092-7483-4

109. FREAKY LANDS, ISBN: 978-1-4092-7603-6

110. TREE SPIRIT, ISBN: 978-1-326-29231-7

111. MAN AND HIS MULE, ISBN: 978-1-291-27090-7

112. LITTLE HUT BY THE SEA, ISBN: 978-1-4478-4066-4

Andreas Sofroniou

Andreas Sofroniou

9 798728 850663